EVERYTHING EXISTS TO RETURN YOU HOME TO LOVE

BROOKE NOVICK

ISBN (Paperback): 979-8-9932840-3-3

ISBN (eBook): 979-8-9932840-8-8

Printed in the United States of America

Cover design by Kristen Paige Andrews

First Edition

Brooke's website: www.brookenovick.com

To Love, with love.
Thank you.

CONTENTS

Introduction   xi

1. Every Aspect of Your Life Is Here to Support Your
   Healing and Evolution   1
2. There Is a Master Plan at Play Here, Even When
   You Cannot Understand It   4
3. The Journey of the Soul   7
4. Love Is the Highest Frequency   9
5. Love Is Real, All Else Is Illusion   11
6. Existence Is Eternal   13
7. You Are Welcome Here Exactly as You Are   14
8. You Are a Miracle   16
9. You Are Nature   19
10. You Are Not Your Body   22
11. Ask for Help, From God and Others   25
12. Honor Both Your Psychological and Spiritual
    Healing   28
13. Feel Your Feelings   32
14. On Trauma and Grief   39
15. Anxiety and Depression Are Symptoms and Not
    the Root of Your Pain   45
16. A Balanced Nervous System Supports the
    Evolution of Your Soul   50
17. Resentment Points to Pain Within   61
18. Treat Yourself with Compassion   64
19. Forgiveness Is the Way to Peace and Freedom   68
20. Purification Returns You to Your True Nature   75
21. The Ego Speaks First, the Soul Speaks Second   78
22. Your External World Reflects Your Internal World   83
23. Nothing Outside You Can Save You   88
24. What You Give, You Receive   91
25. Suffering Is Universal   95
26. Any Energy You Can Be Aware of in Another Also
    Exists Within You   99
27. Those Who Hurt Others Are Hurting   102

28. Hardship Is Designed to Support Your Evolution 105

29. Rejection Is a Blessing in Disguise 109

30. Lessons Continue to Repeat and Grow Louder Until They Are Learned 113

31. Find a Practice That Supports You in Returning Home To Love 117

32. Practice Accepting the Present Moment Instead of Resisting It 121

33. Practice Allowing Others to Be as They Are 124

34. Space, Stillness, and Silence Are Medicines That Help You Return Home to Truth and Love 127

35. Acknowledgment Is a Practice of Devotion 130

36. Prayer Is a Doorway to the Divine 133

37. Offer Your Actions to God 137

38. Live Your Dharma 141

39. Take Responsibility in Your Life 146

40. Honor the Truth of Your Soul 152

41. Your Truth Is Sacred 156

42. You Are Not the Doer 161

43. Surrender Is the Way Home 164

44. Divine Timing Cannot Be Rushed, but You Can Trust it Wholeheartedly 170

45. Trust Periods of Complete Unknown 172

46. You Need Only Know the Next Step 175

47. Fear Is a Threshold Guardian 178

48. When a Challenge Arises, Hand the Situation Over to God 181

49. Peace and Joy Come from Within 184

50. The Only Relationships You Can Control Are the Ones You Have with Yourself and God 187

51. You Had the Family You Needed to Initiate Your Soul's Journey in This Lifetime 190

52. Relationships Are a Vehicle for the Evolution of Your Soul 194

53. Interactions with Others Exist to Support Your Evolution and Return Home to Love 199

54. Practice Resolving Conflict with Compassion and Respect 202

55. When You Hurt Another, You Hurt a Part of Yourself 208

56. Love Does Not Exclude 213

57. Treat Other Beings as You Wish to Be Treated,
    Including Yourself   217
58. Miracles Are Natural   221
59. Your Dream Is Your Destiny   223
60. Let Your Light Shine   226
61. On Death and Dying   230
62. True Liberation Occurs Through the Heart   233
63. On Grace   236
64. Your Life Is a Dream that Exists to Awaken You 240
65. Everything Exists to Return You Home to Love   243
66. Epilogue   248

    Prayers   249
    A Prayer for All Beings   255
    Suggested Reading   257
    Acknowledgments   259
    About the Author   261

"If you descend to the uttermost depths, there you will find the gem of Love."
—*Ramakrishna*

INTRODUCTION

Welcome.

This book has found its way into your life in divine timing and with great purpose.

These writings have arrived to awaken an ancient knowing deep within you, to help you remember that which your soul has always known.

As you move throughout these pages, you will be guided back to the universal wisdom and divine love that are the supreme truth of your being.

In today's fast-paced world, many of us have lost touch with virtues, nature, and love. Modern culture has drifted from community, ritual, and the wisdom of elders, placing productivity above presence, wealth above well-being, and status above service. It is no wonder that so many people feel anxious, isolated, and disconnected from the sacredness of life.

When the ego leads, suffering takes hold; but when truth is honored and love guides the way, peace and miracles unfold.

This book has entered your life to help you remember and reconnect you with your true nature, and to awaken your awareness of the Love within and all around you. It is here to help you shift your perception from fear to love, so you may recognize that everything in your life exists to support you.

What I share here is the wisdom I have been blessed to receive in my own life; truths that have profoundly transformed the way I see both my inner and outer worlds. I am not the source of this wisdom, but rather a vessel through which it has been synthesized and offered to you. I continue to live and integrate these teachings, one day at a time, right alongside you.

At times, these writings may challenge what you feel to be true in your own life and that is okay. There is never pressure to align with anything in this book unless you desire to.

This book is not a replacement for trauma-focused care and is meant to enhance and enrich an already ongoing journey of healing on all levels. Please be sure you have the support you need on your path. You are not meant to navigate life alone.

The wisdom shared here is never offered to pull you away from your human experience, but rather to provide you with a lens with which to view the circumstances of your life from the perspective of the soul. Universal wisdom can support you in seeing your reality differently: zooming out to see the bigger picture and deeper purpose, while still showing up for the totality of your life, one moment at a time.

This book is a companion designed to be read and worked with however you choose; whether you read it in order or not is completely up to you. Allow your intuition to guide you.

Return to these pages whenever you need support grounding back into truth and love.

The passages are intentionally simple and direct, allowing you to absorb their wisdom with ease and integrate them into your daily life at your own pace.

Each section in the book begins with a quote from an enlightened being, revered teacher, or channeled text. When a quotation comes from a channeled text, such as *A Course in Miracles*, the attribution is given to the text itself rather than to the individual who channeled it.

When the word God appears in the book, it is always meant to be spiritual and not religious. The word God here is interchangeable with Love. Please use the word for this term that resonates most for you as you move throughout the book. You will notice the word "love" written with both a capital and lowercase L. Capitalized "Love" refers to the Divine, while lowercase "love" denotes the human emotional experience.

The sacred truths this book shares are the foundations I live by. They have allowed me to navigate challenges with greater acceptance, surrender, and peace. They have deepened my faith and filled my life with a well of trust. They have helped me to see the sacredness in daily life and recognize how perfectly everything is designed to support our healing and evolution.

This wisdom has returned me to the knowing that we live in a loving universe, that love is the foundation of all things, and that everything serves the ultimate purpose of returning us home to Love.

It is my great honor and absolute joy to share this book with you in the prayer that it serves you on your journey.

Please remember: You are human. You will not do any of this perfectly. A commitment to see or act differently can be made in a holy instant, but change often occurs gradually over time, through the habits you consistently practice, one day at a time. The following chapters are not rigid rules, but rather gentle guides to help you walk through life with greater peace, freedom, and love.

I thank you wholeheartedly for welcoming this book and its teachings into your life. Peace in the world begins with peace in our hearts.

May this book help you remember the supreme truth and universal wisdom you already carry within.

May it guide you home to the well of compassion within your heart and the Love that you truly are.

EVERY ASPECT OF YOUR LIFE IS HERE TO SUPPORT YOUR HEALING AND EVOLUTION

*"Your ordinary life is the most perfect ashram you could ever be within.
It is the holy city to which it is wise to make pilgrimage every day."*
—The Way of the Heart

YOUR LIFE IS a vehicle through which you are evolving.

Evolution involves your healing and growth, which bring forth greater wisdom, maturity, and compassion.

While evolution is seldom easy and can feel like everything is ending, it is the very reason you are here and why you have taken this birth.

Evolution always leads you home to wholeness, truth, and Love.

Your soul is a pure spark of the Divine, created by and of the source of all of creation.

Your soul is truth.

Your soul is love.

The present challenge of human existence is that we have forgotten who we are and where we come from. We have forgotten the truth of our being and the love that we are.

The ego believes it is separate from the source of all of creation. Because the ego is built on this illusion, it is often very afraid.

However, fear is not meant to lead.

That is what love is for.

Fear is illusion, love is real.

Everything that arises in your life is here to help you remember and return home to Love.

Challenges never arise without deep purpose.

Challenges arise to guide you towards the very healing your soul came to do in this lifetime.

They arise as a result of your karma, from past actions and past lives, now unfolding in your present birth.

Difficult karma is never punishment, but rather an experience you must navigate in order to heal and grow.

You took this birth to evolve, and that includes the suffering you experience. The pain is part of your curriculum.

As the great saints and sages teach, suffering exists to bring us closer to God.

Suffering, and the desperate longing for it to end, can initiate profound levels of healing and spiritual growth on the human journey.

It is always darkest before the dawn.

Challenges arise to support the liberation of your soul.

As you navigate hardship, remember there is deep purpose in it all.

Grounding into faith during challenging times helps you to keep going, one moment at a time, until you return to the peace that you are once again.

Even when challenges seem senseless, without a thread of hope or meaning, there is divine purpose inherent in them, far beyond what the human mind can fathom.

Pain exists to bring you closer to that which is eternal, to the source of who and what you are.

You are never alone, and Love is always here to guide you.

THERE IS A MASTER PLAN AT PLAY HERE, EVEN WHEN YOU CANNOT UNDERSTAND IT

"It is better to see God in everything than to try and figure it out."
—*Neem Karoli Baba*

EVERYTHING EXISTS WITH PURPOSE.

The purpose is always love.

When life feels overwhelming and nothing seems to make any sense, remember there is a master plan at play here.

When your heart aches and you cannot see a way forward, remember there is a master plan at play here.

The ego believes it knows best, but it does not.

The ego is the aspect of you that believes it is separate from Source; the part that identifies with your body, thoughts, emotions, worldly roles, and personality.

The ego is the aspect of you that has forgotten truth and forsaken faith.

The dimension of you that identifies with the transient nature of being.

The ego is under the spell of the illusion of separateness, yet even the ego is part of the dance of creation.

Nothing stands apart from this dance; there are merely aspects of being that have forgotten supreme truth and ultimate love.

Whatever life may hand you to navigate is always for the highest good of your soul.

The mind never knows better than the ever-present, boundless, and eternal Divine.

This does not imply there will not be pain, but there is always purpose in the pain, even when it seems utterly impossible and entirely unimaginable to comprehend.

This does not mean there is any rush to find meaning when faced with great hardship. There is none at all.

The way out is through, one moment and one breath at a time.

Your evolution cannot be forced. Move at your own pace and trust your process.

More will be revealed in time.

Divine Love knows exactly what is needed for the evolution your soul desires.

You will be carried to and through the exact experiences you need to assist you on your journey home to Love.

You need not try to force, control, or manipulate the situation.

You are exactly where you are supposed to be.

You are held, you are loved, and you are being guided.

There is purpose in it all.

It is far beyond the ability of the human mind to grasp the perfection of the divine plan at play, but it is not for the mind to understand.

The mind craves the familiar, the known, and that which it can control, but God's plan is anything but that.

There is mystery inherent in this being human.

As your faith deepens, so do the blessings you receive.

You must believe in that which you cannot see in order to see it.

When you trust, surrender, and allow yourself to be carried by the great mystery, you begin to see that you are always exactly where you are meant to be.

THE JOURNEY OF THE SOUL

"We are on a long journey, birth to birth to birth."
—*Neem Karoli Baba*

YOUR SOUL HAS BEEN ON, and is presently on, an infinite journey —one that involves all your past lives and experiences of existence.

This present incarnation is but one stop on the journey of your soul.

It is here to help you awaken.

It is here to help you grow.

It continuously presents you with opportunities to get free.

Use your life to remember who you are.

Use your life to remember truth.

Use your life to return home to Love.

Every day is a grand invitation to go beyond the dream of separation and return to that which is eternal.

Every moment is perfectly designed to support you in evolving in the exact ways your soul desires.

You are infinite, unchanging, and luminous.

You are holy and pristine.

You are formless, boundless, and eternal.

You are everlasting.

This is all a dream to carry you home—each lifetime building seamlessly upon the last, divinely guiding you exactly where you are meant to be.

Every minute, every hour, and every day, cosmically crafted with supreme perfection to help you remember and return home to Love.

LOVE IS THE HIGHEST FREQUENCY

"Love is the strongest medicine."
—Neem Karoli Baba

LOVE IS THE HIGHEST FREQUENCY.

There is no energy more powerful than love.

Love can soothe, nourish, and calm.

Love can cleanse, bless, and nurture.

There is nothing that love cannot heal.

If the fearful thoughts of the mind understood the power of love, they would cease to exist.

Love can protect you when you are afraid.

When you ground your being into love, perhaps through thought, prayer, or song, you are protected.

When you focus on love, you are safe, because there is nothing more powerful than love.

Love is a miracle.

Love is the ultimate medicine.

People heal when they are loved.

People are fulfilled when they love.

Love is understanding that we are all one.

Love is seeing nothing but the One.

Love is that which cannot be described.

Love is that from which you came, that which you are made of, and that which guides you in each and every moment.

Love is why you are here and what you are on a journey to remember.

Love is the truth of your being and the foundation of all of existence.

Fear is illusion, love is real.

Allow yourself to be grounded in love, guided by love, and aligned with love.

When love is your north star, your compassion, connection, and devotion deepen every day.

Love is a miracle, and miracles come from love.

LOVE IS REAL, ALL ELSE IS ILLUSION

"There is Bliss and Bliss alone."
—Anandamayi Ma

THIS IS A LOVING universe that exists to return you home to Love.

Love is the foundation of all that you are and all that you experience.

Love is what created you, Love is what you are made of, and Love is why you are here.

Love is real, all else is illusion.

The ego is powerfully committed to its belief in separation, but separation is illusion.

What arises from ego, such as fear, judgement, guilt, and shame, is not ultimate truth.

What arises from love, such as compassion, trust, peace, and faith, is true.

What is rooted in love is real.

What is rooted in love is truth.

Fear is illusion, love is real.

You were created by Love to remember love.

You were created by Love to be love.

Let yourself be guided by that which is real.

Let yourself be guided by the truth of what you are.

You are pure.

You are eternal.

You are source incarnate.

You are Love.

The foundation of all of existence is Love.

EXISTENCE IS ETERNAL

"The Self can never be lost."
—*Ramana Maharshi*

EXISTENCE IS ETERNAL; your current incarnation is not.

Your present form will dissolve; the truth of your being will not.

The love you are is infinite; this incarnation is finite.

Carry these truths with you to more deeply appreciate the present moment.

YOU ARE WELCOME HERE
EXACTLY AS YOU ARE

"You are loved just for being who you are, just for existing."
—*Ram Dass*

YOU ARE WELCOME HERE, for you are a miracle.

With all of your feelings, thoughts, and experiences.

Your darkest shadows along with the divine essence of your truest being.

You are welcome here.

All of you.

There is not one aspect of you the Divine does not love.

For all you have done or not done, said or not said, felt or not felt…

All of you is welcome here.

You are exactly who you have been created to be.

You need not hide even the darkest corners of your inner world.

May you allow yourself to be embraced by the Love that guides you.

May you allow yourself to be held in the arms of Love.

You are welcome here, and you are wholly and completely loved.

You are worthy because you exist.

You are loved because you exist.

You are loved because you are part of the manifestation of God.

You exist because you are loved.

You exist beyond form because you are Love.

YOU ARE A MIRACLE

"Within you is the light of a thousand suns. Within you is unimaginable beauty." —Robert Adams

YOUR BEAUTY and worth are inherent simply because you exist.

To believe you are less than or better than anyone else is illusion.

We are all sparks of the same divine light.

Each being a creation of pure Love itself.

No one is better than or less than anyone else.

No one more worthy or sacred than another.

The ego may try to convince you otherwise, but unloving thoughts are not rooted in truth.

You know illusion by how it feels.

You know truth by how it feels.

The truth is that we are all one.

When you spiral into feelings of shame or unworthiness, that is not truth.

When you feel superior to another, that too is untrue.

You may be farther along on your path, but the destination is the same for us all.

Comparison is a tactic of the ego, attempting either to make you feel superior to relieve shame or inferior to keep you small.

The ego, ever fearful of vanishing, employs countless tricks to create a false sense of safety.

One of those tricks is telling you that you are not good enough or that you are less worthy than another.

The ego runs on fear. It does not understand that it is safe to be who you are and shine your divine light.

When you believe you are less than, you undermine the holy creation of Divine Love that you are.

You forget that you are one with all, that everyone is part of you, and you are part of everyone.

This human journey is not about being perfect. It is about being who you are.

It is natural to make mistakes.

It is natural to do things you wish you had not done.

It is natural to have moments you wish you had handled differently.

None of this diminishes your inherent worth.

It is the nature of the ego to sometimes compare, criticize, or condemn.

To think thoughts of inadequacy or pride.

None of this is who you are.

None of this is your true nature.

Missteps on the path are part of being human.

They are part of how we learn.

None of these moments define you.

None of them diminish the miracle that you are.

This human journey is not designed to be navigated with perfection, but rather to teach you how to repair, resolve, and continuously return back home to Love.

This applies not only to your relationships with others but, first and foremost, to the relationship you have with yourself.

Anything that comes from Love is a miracle.

You were created by Love.

You are created of Love.

You are a holy miracle of Love.

YOU ARE NATURE

"Nature is our first mother. She nurtures us throughout our lives. Our birth mother may allow us to sit on her lap for a couple of years, but Mother Nature patiently bears our weight our entire life."
—*Amma*

You are woven of stars.

The same stardust that composes the elements also composes your entire human body.

The same life force that lives in the trees also lives within you.

The boundless, radiant, and infinite Love that created everything in existence is who you truly are.

Nonetheless, many people are profoundly disconnected from nature, and in turn, their true nature.

In the busyness of modern daily life, we rarely make time to listen to the breeze blowing through the leaves or lie upon the earth to gaze at a sky full of stars. We forget these are the true measures of wealth.

We are disconnected from nature and the love that we are.

We have forgotten one another.

We have forgotten the Divine Mother.

So, what can be done?

Do that which returns you to your true nature.

Spend time outside.

Dance or move your body in harmony with the earth.

Sing from your heart to the animals and plants.

Sit outside for an evening by the fire.

You can listen to the heartbeat of a tree, receive the wisdom of the river, and allow the wind to clear away everything within you that is not love.

Create to connect with the energy that flows through all things.

Connect with that which inherently abides within your heart.

You are nature.

The reason it feels so magnificently nourishing to connect with the earth, air, water, and fire is because the elements are ancient and holy medicines for humans.

The elements are divinely designed to heal and support you. They return you to your true nature and lead you from ego to soul.

Supporting yourself with the elements can be such a simple yet profound practice.

Breathing in fresh air, placing your feet upon the earth, lighting a candle, or bathing are all simple ways to bring the elements into your daily life.

The more connected to the elements you are, the more grounded, nourished, and healed you will feel.

Connecting to nature supports you in experiencing innate peace and love, which exist beyond inner and outer circumstances.

Nature holds the support you seek.

Nature reminds you of the wisdom you carry within.

Mother Earth is available to ground, nurture, and hold you.

She is available to cleanse, heal, and nourish you.

Nature returns you to that which you are and that which created you.

Nature returns you to your true nature and returns you home to Love.

YOU ARE NOT YOUR BODY

"Accept this identification only: that you are pure beingness, the very soul of the universe, and that for now you are just wearing this bodily attire." —Nisargadatta Maharaj

YOU ARE NOT YOUR BODY.

Bodies are born and bodies die.

You are that which remains.

You are pure awareness.

You are eternal.

You are not the youth of the body.

You are not the decaying of the body.

You are not the wrinkles.

You are not the graying hair.

You are not the aging of the body.

Bodies decay.

That's what they do.

Clinging to form causes suffering.

Clinging to that which is impermanent causes sorrow.

Allowing what is returns you to truth.

Surrendering to what is returns you to peace.

Take a deep breath and bring your focus from your mind into your heart.

Connect with the consciousness and loving awareness that you are.

The body is not the truth of who you are.

The body is the temporary home of your soul.

You are a celestial being in a body.

You are Love embodied.

You are presence.

You are consciousness.

You are everlasting loving awareness.

Bodies come and bodies go.

You are not your body.

You are something far greater, more expansive, and completely transcendent.

You are boundless, formless, and unchanging love.

You are infinite.

You are that which exists beyond being and non-being.

Your body is sacred, as it allows you to live out your incarnation, evolve, and grow closer to Love each day.

It is beautiful to care for and respect your body, but remember always, it is not who you are.

You are not your body.

The body is finite.

You are infinite.

The body is transient.

You are eternal.

The bodies dies.

You do not.

Let the body do what it must do.

It is not designed to last forever.

Your body is a temporary aspect of this temporary dream.

You were created by Love, you are Love, and you will always be Love.

You will never not be.

You will always be.

You are eternal.

You are loving awareness.

You are everlasting.

ASK FOR HELP, FROM GOD AND OTHERS

"He grants and will grant His touch in His own time. But we have to do our duty, which is to call out to Him. You must do your own work. He will look after His." —Anandamayi Ma

DIVINE LOVE IS ALWAYS available to call upon and ask for help.

Divine Love is always present and ready to assist you.

Often the ego leads you to believe that you know best, which causes you to ask the universe for what your ego desires. Then, when you do not receive it, you believe God has failed you in some way.

This is pure illusion.

This is false.

The mind does not know better than Love.

If something does not come to you, it is always, without doubt, for your highest and greatest good.

The Divine desires to assist you in every single moment, but you must first sincerely ask for the help you desire.

Just as a mother tending to her child answers the call of a sincere cry, the Divine responds when you earnestly call upon it.

The ways in which your prayers are answered may not align with how your ego wishes them to be, but you can rest assured that you always receive exactly what is needed in each and every moment.

What you receive is precisely what you need to assist with your healing and evolution at this time.

Pray with respect for that which you are praying to.

Ask for help whenever you need it.

Love desires to help you always.

You need not limit your prayers, for Love is infinite and only deepens the more you connect with it.

When challenging thoughts, emotions, or experiences arise, pray.

Hand them over to God.

Ask for help.

You are not alone, and you need not carry the burden alone.

God desires to carry it for you, but you must first earnestly ask for help.

You are not designed to navigate this life alone. Beyond asking the Divine for assistance, it is beautiful to be held by trusted others, as well.

Surrounding yourself with support allows you to receive miracles through others.

Asking for help is an act of sheer humility, courage, and strength.

Asking for help allows you to open to and receive the grace of God.

You are not meant to navigate life alone.

Allow yourself to be held.

Receive the support you are worthy of, and as you do, watch the peace, power, and love that awakens within and all around you.

HONOR BOTH YOUR PSYCHOLOGICAL AND SPIRITUAL HEALING

"Each act becomes part of the awakening."
—Ram Dass

As a human with an ego, nurturing both your psychological and spiritual healing is essential.

When you bypass the psychological and focus only on the spiritual, you can miss out on the profound healing, wisdom, and transformation you took this birth to experience.

By avoiding earthly challenges, you skip over key aspects of evolution that require your active participation.

Your evolution becomes built on a foundation made of sand, because the difficulties and pain you are being called to face and grow from are being denied.

This can look like spending significant amounts of time in meditation, but not allowing yourself to acknowledge pain within and feel your feelings.

This can also look like using spiritual truths to avoid difficult conversations or setting boundaries.

Using your pain to help you grow supports you in evolving, opening your heart, and deepening your wisdom.

It assists you in expanding your compassion and grounding more deeply into love.

When you allow the challenges of life to support your healing, you access the transformation available to you through your daily life.

You access the wealth of grace available to assist in your awakening each day.

Conversely, when your focus rests solely on the psychology of the mind, you can miss out on the miracle of existence itself.

You bypass the experience of that which is greater than the mind, that which you truly are.

You miss that which cannot be known, only experienced.

You miss the miracles that Love has to offer.

This can look like intensely analyzing your mind and actions, constantly thinking, interpreting, and labeling, but not allowing yourself to travel beyond the realm of the mind and simply rest in the seat of your heart.

For the Divine is beyond all thought and words.

It must be experienced.

When you honor your true nature and the nature of all of existence, you are able to move through the world more deeply grounded in love.

You become grounded in truth and guided by that which is real.

You embody the knowing that we are all one and that everything arises to support your awakening.

Your spiritual evolution supports you in releasing illusion and remembering truth.

Both paths of healing exist because each one serves your liberation.

What is skipped over in one lifetime can simply arise in another.

The opportunity for evolution forever presents itself.

Honoring both your humanness and your soul is a continual practice. By focusing your awareness on each realm, you are able to care for and tend to your needs each day.

When you notice resistance within one or both planes of evolution, be gentle with yourself, for there is always a reason for this fear.

The awareness of the resistance is enough to help you go beyond it.

When you begin to experience the gifts that healing on each level offers, you begin to feel more willing to honor both planes.

You begin to desire the healing each has to offer and the miracles they can deliver to your life.

The human journey is a spiritual experience; the two are forever intertwined.

Healing on both the psychological and spiritual levels allows you to receive the deepest amount of evolution in your sacred incarnation.

It supports you in living the highest octave of your present birth and sets you up well for your next one.

When you honor healing on multiple planes of existence, you honor the truth of who you are.

You are spirit in a body.

You are source incarnate.

You are both human and soul.

Ego and Divine Love.

You are a beautiful human, and you are an absolute miracle of existence.

FEEL YOUR FEELINGS

"The pain is an inevitable part of the journey, but it will not last."
—*Neem Karoli Baba*

FEELING your feelings is a fundamental part of being human.

Allowing yourself to be present with, feel, and release a feeling is a sacred act, one that honors the holy human experience you came here to have.

Pain cannot be bypassed, but it can be suppressed, repressed, minimized, and denied.

The avoidance of pain only causes it to be expressed elsewhere, in more distressing and destructive ways.

The avoidance of pain only causes more pain.

That said, resistance to emotions is as natural as having them, and resistance often comes before you allow yourself to feel. This, too, is part of the human experience.

However resistance shows up, its job is always the same: to assist you in avoiding what is vulnerable or that which the mind deems uncomfortable, unbearable, or uncontrollable.

When resistance leads, it brings with it even greater pain, but the moment you recognize it, name it, and accept yourself in it, you evolve and begin to move beyond it.

What becomes repressed by the ego is not bad; it simply asks to be seen, acknowledged, and accepted in the light of awareness. Once it is, any shame, fear, or guilt connected to what has been pushed away can begin to dissolve.

Resistance can be extremely painful, yet it may also generate the very suffering needed to propel you forward.

When you move through resistance and allow yourself to be present with what is, you come out on the other side more clear, authentic, and liberated.

Feeling supports you in releasing that which you are not meant to carry. It lightens the load and purifies your entire being.

You emerge more deeply connected to God.

Feeling feelings that have been long suppressed can bring deep discomfort, but every single moment you feel and allow the emotions within you to exist, you release the heavy burden that carrying their weight around brings.

If you fear that the feelings, darkness, and discomfort will never end, know that there will come a time when the lightness and light of your true being will return.

Being present with pain is a significant part of healing.

Being present with pain is a spiritual act.

Being present with pain is a significant part of the path towards embodying universal truths like acceptance, forgiveness, and oneness.

Such truths, however, remain completely out of reach until you give yourself space to feel and allow that which is within you to be experienced and released.

Your feelings are valid simply because they exist. They do not always mean what your mind may tell you they mean, but they always require your attention, acknowledgment, and love.

It is essential to learn how to acknowledge and process your emotions in ways that are safe and supportive for you and others.

Pain begins to heal the moment you acknowledge it and allow it to move through you.

Every time you feel your feelings, you receive a healing.

Every time you feel your feelings, you purify your entire being.

Feeling your feelings supports you in evolving.

Feeling your feelings supports you in opening your heart and returning home to Love.

We are all asked to navigate uncomfortable feelings and painful emotions, and while this experience can sometimes feel terrible or debilitating, feeling the pain allows us to heal and evolve in the ways our souls desire.

When you do not feel what wants to be felt, you are left in an even greater state of pain than before.

When you push your feelings away, distressing and unwanted symptoms arise.

When the energy of a feeling is suppressed, it merely expresses itself elsewhere.

The ego will try everything in its power to avoid feeling, but this only causes more pain over time.

Feeling is the most direct route to healing.

What you resist, persists.

What you feel, heals.

When feelings are not felt, they become a heaviness you are forced to carry.

Holding them inside drains energy, energy that could be expressed more freely or creatively in your life.

The extra weight of feelings unfelt impacts many different aspects of life, including your thoughts, perception, choices, mood, vitality, and more.

The mind may believe that feeling requires time you do not have, but feeling need not take very long. Even a few minutes of being present with your inner world and allowing your feelings to move through you can be absolutely profound, especially when done regularly.

You do not always need to understand what caused the feelings you are experiencing. Your emotions may arise in response to something within you, another person, in relationship, or simply from the pain inherent in the human experience.

It is okay if you do not have clarity on the root of your feelings. The feelings simply ask that you feel them, and in doing so, you open a doorway to what is needed next.

When you allow your emotions to move through you, you release that which you no longer need to carry.

When you allow your emotions to move through you, you process pain and create space for truth to be revealed.

When you allow your emotions to move through you, you purify your entire being.

It is essential to remember that while the circumstances in your life exist to return you home to Love, the feelings that arise from your experiences yearn to be acknowledged, accepted, and felt.

There are many ways that we may unconsciously avoid our feelings.

The mind may engage in busyness, over-thinking, or escapism.

It may fixate on things outside itself, like other people or events.

The mind may even stealthily use spiritual truths to evade feelings. This can sound like saying, "Everything happens for a reason," or, "This is just my past karma playing out," in such a way that represses the pain associated with what happened.

Feeling is a powerful act of vulnerability, which the ego enormously fears. It does not understand that it is safe to be vulnerable.

While feeling is fundamental to health on all levels, it is also important to find balance and not completely lose yourself or drown in your emotions.

If your emotions are keeping you from the roles and responsibilities of daily life, you can see this as an opportunity to receive support, be held, and find your way to greater groundedness.

Feeling is especially important when moving through a challenging time. Equally as essential is allowing yourself to be nurtured and cared for throughout your experience.

Having someone by your side who you trust and feel safe with, and who treats you with compassion and respect, can be an excellent way to be supported in this stage of your evolution.

If you have a difficult time recognizing or feeling your feelings, that is okay. Offer yourself compassion, for there are entirely understandable reasons you learned to cope in this way.

Ways of coping that once served to protect you as a child can unintentionally cause harm and challenges for you as an adult.

If connecting with your emotions feels difficult for you, it will take conscious effort to check in with yourself and create space for your feelings to arise.

They may not emerge right away, as your ego does not yet understand that it is safe for them to do so.

Be patient and gentle with yourself. Once you feel safe enough, what lies within will begin to release.

It is immensely helpful to create space to tend to yourself and allow your feelings to arise.

You can focus on your breath, move your body, vocalize your emotions, or listen to emotionally evocative music to help your feelings move.

Over time, you will learn to recognize when you have feelings that want to be felt and will know how to best support yourself in feeling them. The more you practice this, the easier it will become.

Acknowledging and feeling the emotions within you supports you in releasing the heaviness of being human, while simultaneously creating space for deeper peace, freedom, and connection to Self.

Feeling the emotions within you is sacred. It is surrender. It is the bravest of the brave.

Acknowledging what lies within is a holy act.

It is in deepest alignment with Love's will for you.

You know this by the sense of purification that feeling brings—the feeling of having touched divine truth after dropping the walls around your heart and allowing emotion to move through you.

You know this by what happens when you go beyond the thinking mind and enter the realm of the heart—when there is nothing standing in between you and your inner world.

It is a spiritual act to acknowledge, feel, and give space to what desires to be experienced through the light of your awareness.

When you feel, you evolve.

Every time you feel your feelings, you courageously show up for the experience of life being offered to you.

Every time you feel your feelings, you allow life force energy to move through you unobstructed.

Every time you feel your feelings, you support all of existence in returning home to Love.

ON TRAUMA AND GRIEF

"Always remember that when dusk arrives, it already has dawn in its womb." —Amma

SOME EXPERIENCES in life simply cannot be rushed.

The healing of trauma and the journey through grief are such experiences.

These processes are portals—

Of descent, dissolution, and destruction,

Of initiation, regeneration, and rebirth.

Once they have begun, you will never again be the same person as before.

When the pain is immense and suffering takes hold, know that you are not alone.

When the challenges of life feel far too enormous to navigate, know that you are where Love needs you to be.

When tragedy, crisis, or profound loss arrives, surrender yourself at the feet of the Mother of the Universe.

Allow her to embrace you in unconditional love, for you are never too much of anything for her.

Offer her your suffering, shock, and rage,

Your weeping, loneliness, and denial.

She will hold you through the resistance and returning, the forgetting and remembering.

This level of pain, though so very deep and all-encompassing, is not permanent.

Meeting it, one moment at a time and at your own pace, is exactly what allows it to shift and transform over time.

Grief is not limited to death only, though death is certainly one experience that can powerfully evoke it.

Grief is universal and can arise for many different reasons.

Loss of identity, loss of a chapter of life, loss of a dream, loss of a home, loss of a relationship, and so on.

The thread that weaves through them all is loss.

Loss is inherent in the human experience.

Even when you feel ready for a new chapter to begin, grief can still be present, as experiencing mixed feelings is perfectly natural.

You can also experience grief on a collective level.

Grief for the suffering of the world, grief for the creatures whose needs go unmet, and grief for our beloved Mother Earth.

When grief is not allowed—when it is pushed away, denied, or numbed—we become disconnected from our hearts.

Grief is given to us to support us in becoming emptier, stronger, and more heart-centered.

Grief brings with it an offering of wisdom.

Grief brings with it an offering of truth.

Suffering opens, humbles, and purifies the heart.

It dissolves the illusions of the ego and helps us to rest in the seat of the soul.

Immense sorrow can heal the parts of you that have disconnected from truth and forgotten Love.

This level of healing asks you to meet the pain, one moment and one breath at a time, as often as you are able.

There will be times when you are unable to, and that is okay.

There will be days when you feel you cannot go on, yet somehow miraculously you will.

There will be times when all you can do is make it through the day, and that is a victory to be acknowledged.

This level of pain will not last forever.

The abyss of nothingness, suffering, or heartache will transform over time.

Every single time you meet the pain, if even for a moment, you bring it into the light of awareness to be transformed.

Every time you sit with the incredible wounding or sorrow, you allow it to exist and therefore heal.

The pain within you requires space to move through you in its own time.

Practice letting it.

Practice allowing the fear, doubt, and confusion.

The sorrow, disillusionment, and despair.

Healing happens every time you allow yourself to feel.

Every time you allow yourself to be as you are.

To be where you are.

Healing happens in the present moment.

Let it be okay to feel how you feel.

Allow and accept the feelings.

Allow and feel the feelings.

This is part of the holy process of healing you have been placed in.

This is part of your courageous journey of destruction and rebirth.

The rage, resistance, and revulsion.

The unfamiliar, unknown, and unclear.

It is all a step on the path to liberation.

It is all a step on the pathway home to Love.

Dark nights require deep support so you may be held in the unraveling, the questioning, and the despair.

There is never any rush or pressure in these portals of pain to make meaning or prematurely pursue spiritual ideals like acceptance, understanding, or forgiveness.

Such virtues can only be accessed by meeting the pain that arises within you.

The way out is through.

Your process cannot be rushed, but it can be deeply supported.

This terrain is not meant to be navigated alone.

It is imperative that you are held and cared for in your experience.

Ask for help from the Divine and from others.

Each person will navigate these experiences in their own unique way, and it is essential to honor however you are called to do so, as long as you are safe and supported in your process.

You may feel everything all at once.

You may feel nothing at all.

Whatever arises, practice meeting it with acceptance.

Practice meeting it with compassion.

The way out of the pain is to move through it, one moment and one breath at a time.

There are no shortcuts, but there are ways to be nurtured, held, and guided along the way.

Because the purpose of suffering is to bring you into deeper union with Love, your relationship with the Divine can offer profound support during times of crisis and upheaval.

Ask for help and allow Divine Love to carry you.

Your connection with the Divine is meant to support you throughout your entire life, especially during the most challenging parts of it.

Suffering exists with purpose.

Suffering is a pathway home to that which never dies and that which is never born.

Suffering is a pathway home to that which is eternal. The space beyond form and formlessness, birth and death, reality and illusion.

Healing is not linear.

There will be moments that feel like complete setbacks and days when you cannot get out of bed. These days, however, are not defeats at all. They are part of your healing, part of your remembering, and part of your return home to Love.

Let your heart break.

Let the pain crack you open so that only love remains.

Bathe yourself in compassion.

Bathe yourself in acceptance for where you are.

Bathe yourself in love.

Your willingness to show up to each new day and each new moment is a sheer act of courage.

This degree of darkness will heal, one breath at a time.

You are divinely held, supported, and guided.

You are exactly where you are supposed to be.

You are never alone in this, not even for one moment.

You are being carried by Love.

You are so deeply loved.

Love is here.

Love is not leaving.

Healing is happening in every moment.

Healing is happening with every breath.

ANXIETY AND DEPRESSION ARE SYMPTOMS AND NOT THE ROOT OF YOUR PAIN

"Every part of the birth you are taking is part of the unfolding of the karma you need to burn through. There is not one experience you are having or could have or have had that is not part of that process."
—Ram Dass

ANXIETY AND DEPRESSION are widespread in our modern world.

Humans once spent most of their days outdoors in community, stewarding the land, singing, dancing, sitting in ceremony, engaging in ritual, learning from elders, meeting with healers, and experiencing rites of passage.

Today, many of us spend much of our time indoors, on screens, disconnected from self, nature, and one another, with no ceremonies, rituals, or elders to guide us.

The systems we live within are not designed to lead us home to Love, but rather away from it.

Society values productivity over presence, and avoidance over feeling.

We do not learn the crucial act of how to meet our feelings and how to allow them to move through us.

We do not learn about compassion, communication, or how to be in relationship with ourselves, one another, and the Earth.

It is no surprise then, that symptoms like anxiety and depression run rampant.

Yet, woven within these deeply painful experiences are the exact circumstances needed to help you heal, grow, and awaken.

Every predicament arises to support you in opening your heart and uncovering the truth of who you are.

These symptoms emerge to support your healing and return home to truth and Love.

Anxiety can manifest in many different forms, including fear, worry, fixation, and more.

No matter the form, anxiety is always an invitation into deeper healing.

It is an invitation into the present moment.

An invitation to be present in your body and with your breath.

Anxiety is an invitation out of your mind and into your heart.

An invitation out of thinking and into feeling.

Anxiety is an invitation to ground into trust, faith, and Divine Love.

The content of anxious thoughts is not what deserves your attention, but rather what are the thoughts attempting to keep you from?

What lies underneath, just beyond the anxiety?

What life force energy within you is yearning to be felt, expressed, or acknowledged?

What are these thoughts trying to keep you from feeling, acknowledging, or being present with?

Anxiety is your mind's misguided attempt to protect you from that which feels vulnerable or that which it cannot control.

When you meet what is underneath the fear with tenderness, you access a sacred wellspring of healing and wisdom within you.

Anxiety often involves over-thinking to avoid feeling, or the intellectualization of your emotions instead of simply feeling them. It is important to recognize when this is happening so you can gently guide yourself back into the present moment, back into your body, and back into feeling.

While anxiety can be immensely uncomfortable, its grip begins to loosen when you begin to meet what lies beneath it.

Doing so is a pathway to surrender.

A pathway home to Love.

Being supported through this experience is essential. Through aligned support you can uncover the source of the symptom, address what it is attempting to communicate, and integrate its teachings to support your healing and evolution.

This allows you to move from fear to love.

Depression, just like anxiety, is not the root of the problem but a symptom pointing to pain within.

Depression can arise for a number of different reasons, including feeling unhappy with life, feeling powerless, or not acknowledging, feeling, or expressing deep pain within.

It can arise when you carry a burden that feels too heavy to hold, when you wear a mask that no longer fits, or when you feel stuck and stagnant and the energy of your spirit yearns to freely express itself.

Depression can arise from feeling disconnected from your true being or the Divine.

It can be a signal of past-life or present-life pain that is seeking resolution, or ancestral pain within the family lineage seeking healing.

When depression arrives, it always does so with great purpose and a message.

The isolation, hopelessness, and despair,

The misery, pain, and sorrow.

Every thread woven with intention,

To help what has been hidden, be seen.

What has been suppressed, to be felt.

And what has been locked away, to be freed.

The brave and karmic voyage into the underworld is here to help you heal in the ways your soul desires.

Can you journey just a step beyond the darkness of the thinking mind and allow yourself to receive the message that awaits you?

Please do not traverse this terrain alone.

Having aligned support is invaluable.

It is deeply important to be held and guided in your process.

When depression leads, it leads you far from home, but when you ask for help and let Love lead the way, you are carried to places you never knew existed.

Depression exists to guide you into the holy fire of transformation.

It is a pathway to surrender, connection, and the Divine.

Depression exists to lead you on a sacred pilgrimage back to yourself, back to truth, and back home to Love.

Depression begins to dissolve once the messages it yearns to communicate have been received, and the necessary changes (whether internal or external) have been set in motion.

When we attempt to heal anxiety and depression without exploring what lies beneath them or what they are attempting to communicate, we place a temporary bandage over a deeper issue that will continue to grow louder until it is acknowledged and addressed.

Anxiety and depression are sacred communicators pointing to something within that is yearning for your attention.

They point to feelings longing to be felt, truths craving to be expressed, or aspects of you aching to be loved.

They point to the need for connection, community, and care.

They lead in the direction of the Divine.

When you accept the invitation these symptoms offer, you become initiated on a journey inward and begin to receive the healing and evolution your soul desires.

Anxiety and depression are not here to punish you; they exist solely to help you.

These symptoms exist to shepherd you towards truth.

These symptoms arise to lead you home to Love.

A BALANCED NERVOUS SYSTEM SUPPORTS THE EVOLUTION OF YOUR SOUL

"When you meet a being who is centered, you always know it. You always feel a kind of calm emanation."
—Ram Dass

A BALANCED NERVOUS system allows you to engage with the world from a grounded place, with a centered presence.

The more peace you cultivate within, the more able you become to steadily traverse the evolutionary terrain of your life.

When you are balanced internally, you are able to navigate challenges and stress with greater ease.

When the body is at peace, the mind can be still.

When the mind is at ease, the body can feel safe.

A serene, spacious mind supports you in making decisions in alignment with truth, intuition, and love.

A regulated nervous system allows you to tune more deeply into what is true.

A regulated system expands your capacity to be a conscious participant in your life.

When your nervous system is activated, whether in fight, flight, freeze, or fawn, your thoughts and thinking become affected.

The thoughts that arise from such a place are rooted in the fearful experience of the body and system.

Urgency, desperation, and dissociation—each one a signal pointing to activation.

Thoughts that arise from fear lead you away from what is true.

Thoughts born of peace lead you gracefully home.

Your true nature is compassionate and pure.

Your true being is formless, boundless love.

Knowing what is causing the activation within and having a pathway to return to balance allows you to heal.

The activation may be a sign to feel feelings, express yourself, or acknowledge a truth.

It may be a sign to slow down, ask for help, or create space for yourself.

The activation may be encouraging you to be honest, set a boundary, or honor your needs.

Activation always arrives with a message.

Tune into what it is communicating to you.

When you navigate the world with a deep connection to the center of your being, you move as Love would have you move.

You think as Love would have you think.

You speak as Love would have you speak.

And you do as Love would have you do.

A dysregulated system can give rise to many things, including physical symptoms, reactivity, addiction, anxiety, depression, and overwhelm.

Worry, volatility, placating, and retreating can all be signs of an activated nervous system.

Periods of prolonged dysregulation close your heart, as your system remains in survival mode. In this state, it becomes difficult to process additional stimuli or emotion. The nervous system must first restore balance, steadiness, and equanimity before having space for the fullness of life once again.

Living from an ungrounded state can cause contraction, constriction, and a closing off to connection and the world.

When we struggle to hold the energy of our own lives, we lose the capacity to be present in the lives of others.

Nourishing connection requires the ability to be present and grounded.

The benefits of a balanced system include increased presence, compassion, and peace. From a centered place, you are able to navigate daily life with greater awareness, integrity, and acceptance. You may even feel relieved or grateful after witnessing how you respond to stress.

A regulated system provides you with a deeper connection to yourself and your needs, a greater ability to speak up and communicate when necessary, and a more nourishing relationship with others and the Divine.

The power of learning how to regulate your nervous system cannot be underestimated. With practice, it becomes easier and more natural over time.

You begin to recognize the subtle or not-so-subtle signs that your system is activated, that you are ungrounded, or that you feel overwhelmed.

You begin to learn what helps you soothe and nurture yourself back to peace.

Maintaining a sense of groundedness and calm involves tending to both the physical and emotional bodies.

As you cultivate peace within your physical body, your emotional body begins to learn that it is safe, as well.

Supporting yourself in feeling emotionally safe is one of the greatest gifts you can offer to your nervous system.

Crying helps you regulate.

Screaming, shaking, and stomping alone in a room helps you regulate.

Releasing what is yearning for your attention within allows your system to regulate.

When your system is activated, it is signaling you to become aware of spaces or experiences that feel unsafe, misaligned, or overwhelming. This is not wrong; this is a miraculous feature of your human body.

It alerts you when you do not honor your truth, emotions, and desires.

It alerts you when you have veered off-path.

Your body lets you know when you have surpassed your limits, and it signals when you require space to tend to your own needs.

The goal is not to be perfectly calm all of the time.

The goal is to become aware of your body, the messages it communicates, and to be able to support yourself in returning to your center.

The goal is to know how to care for yourself in healthy ways as you navigate the experiences of your life.

This might look like creating space to weep or release rage.

This might look like communicating your feelings and needs when necessary.

Or this might look like saying no to that which feels out of alignment.

Feeling and expressing yourself may support you in healing the root of the dysregulation, but it is also important to have practices that create safety in your body and mind once you have become activated. Explore different methods and find what resonates for you.

Perhaps it is relaxing your muscles, taking slow deep breaths, and reminding yourself that you are safe.

Perhaps it is chanting a certain mantra or song.

It may be listening to crystal singing bowls, a grounding meditation, or placing your body upon the earth.

It may be splashing cold water on your face or placing an ice pack on the back of your neck.

It may be offering a sincere prayer from your heart and asking for help.

You may feel called to dim the lights, light a candle, and place selenite upon your chest.

Or perhaps a weighted blanket, lavender eye mask, and body scan are the types of nurturing you seek.

Grounding breaths, soothing sounds, relaxing smells, dim lighting, and aligned sensate support can all be deeply grounding. When the system is overloaded and overwhelmed, tending to your sensory experiences and removing overstimulation can feel exceptionally nourishing.

Working with aligned herbs and minerals can also provide a soothing balm for your system.

When you feel disconnected from your body, the elements can profoundly hold you, ground you, and return you home to presence.

You may feel called to a bath, fire, or gazing up at the starry sky.

Honor what feels supportive and resonant for you.

If you are somewhere where you do not have access to anything but your breath and prayer, that alone is enough.

You can breathe, pray, and return to presence no matter where you are or what you are doing.

The Divine has bestowed these tools upon you, available in every moment of your life.

With these practices, you can be swiftly carried back to presence, back to truth, and back home to Love.

Beyond the ways you can support yourself on your own, remember, you are not meant to navigate the challenges of life alone. Seeking an aligned therapist, healer, teacher, mentor, or support group can offer immense assistance.

Allow yourself to be held and supported on your path with those whom you trust and feel safe with, as doing so can make all the difference.

When you give yourself time and space to be present with your inner world, you meet what is asking for your attention and you help create safety for yourself on all levels.

Learning to care for your nervous system supports you in learning to care for yourself.

You learn to tune into and honor your needs and wishes.

You learn to speak up for yourself and honor your body, mind, heart, spirit, and soul in all the ways Divine Love wants for you.

Caring for your nervous system allows you to support yourself in living as Love wants you to live.

The more aware you become of your nervous system, the more aware you become of your triggers, reactions, and responses to stress.

With practice and time, you are able to notice the presence of stress before a reaction surfaces, which grants you sacred space to tend to yourself and choose how you would like to respond.

A balanced system reduces reactivity and increases aligned responses.

It allows you to move through triggers without harming yourself or others.

The more you tend to your needs in daily life, whether physical, mental, emotional, or spiritual, the less reactive you become. You are able to meet, move through, and let go of stress in the moment, instead of holding onto and carrying it for extended periods of time.

A grounded nervous system allows you to traverse stressful situations, such as having a difficult conversation, receiving upsetting news, or dealing with the grief inherent in being human, in a healthier way.

When you know how to care for your nervous system, saying no when you want to and yes only when you want to also becomes easier.

When you are balanced, you can more fully accept other people's feelings in relation to you, whether disappointment, anger, or frustration, without needing to rush to change, fight, or deny them.

When you are centered, you are able to hold the energy of daily life from a more steady space.

Learning how to care for and soothe your nervous system allows you to expand in ways you could not do otherwise.

When you meet stressful situations from a centered space, you are more able to move through them in ways that expand and evolve you, rather than defeat or drain you.

A centered presence is like a candle's flame. It can illuminate as many other candles as it wishes, without ever diminishing its own light.

A regulated system naturally impacts those around it, helping others to feel more grounded and at peace.

Learning how to regulate your nervous system does not remove the challenges of life, but allows you to navigate them with greater presence, trust, and strength.

Feeling grounded helps your thoughts be rooted in truth, faith, and universal wisdom.

Learning how to care for yourself sets you free in a world that is constantly pushing you further away from yourself, your needs, and the love that is your truest being.

Prioritizing your care, yourself, and your needs in this way may not be understood by everyone, and that is okay. That, too, can become easier to sit with the more you nurture yourself.

Understanding the subtle signs of when you need support helps to prevent greater collapses down the line.

Living from a centered, present space opens you to greater joy, creativity, and connection.

Being grounded in peace allows you to meet the happenings of daily life in presence, with the deeper knowing that you are safe, you are held, and you can do hard things.

A regulated system allows you to move through life with deeply rooted faith.

As your nervous system grows stronger over time, it helps you to feel more confident, capable, and compassionate.

When you are regulated, you have more to give not only to yourself, but to those around you, as well.

A regulated nervous system supports you in communicating with greater ease, clarity, honesty, and respect.

It supports you in accepting what life hands you, and allows life force energy to flow through you unobstructed.

There are simple ways to begin practicing all of this in this very moment.

Take a deep breath into your belly, and exhale.

Check in with the feelings that are present for you right now.

Name them.

Notice how your body feels.

Do you notice any tension or constriction?

Do you feel hot or cold?

Are your muscles tense or relaxed?

Are your thoughts rooted in fear or in love?

Now relax your body, and if it feels comfortable for you, gently close your eyes.

Take a few deep breaths in through your nose and then slowly exhale through your mouth.

When you are ready, notice how you feel after giving yourself just a moment of presence and care.

You are spirit in a body, and your body is on loan for this one lifetime. Your body is the home of your soul, for now, and it allows you to be on this journey of awakening you presently walk. Your body, therefore, asks that you care for, tend to, and honor it.

In doing so, your entire life will benefit.

Begin learning situations that can feel activating, overstimulating, or unsafe for you.

Perhaps it is rushing, being around certain people, or loud noises.

Perhaps it is having triggering conversations, not asking for help, or not having space to yourself on a regular basis.

Begin learning what triggers stress for you and ways to support yourself in those situations. Each person will have access to different resources and support. Tune into what is doable for you.

The Divine gave you this body, mind, nervous system, and life. Whatever your needs are, they are divinely sent.

Love desires for you to honor the needs of your soul; otherwise they would not exist.

Your needs are Spirit.

Your needs are sacred.

Support yourself, nurture yourself, nourish yourself, and soothe yourself.

The more you care for yourself with gentleness, tenderness, and love, the more that tenderness will be reflected back to you.

The more peace you cultivate within, the more peace you promote all around you.

Your true nature is peace.

Your true being is compassion.

The truth of who you are is boundless, formless, and luminous love.

RESENTMENT POINTS
TO PAIN WITHIN

"May your thoughts, words, and actions arise from love."
—Amma

WHEN YOU STEW in frustration or resentment towards another, the energy within the resentment is stuck.

It is unable to move.

When you allow yourself to go beyond the aggravation, you see that this is not mere irritation or annoyance.

At its root, this is pain.

This is anger at feeling disrespected.

This is fear of not being considered.

This is sadness from not feeling connected in the ways you desire.

These feelings arise so that they may be addressed.

They do not want to remain trapped in the cycle of overthinking, rumination, or ego-driven resentment.

These feelings want to be acknowledged and felt.

This pain seeks to guide you towards release, repair, and resolution in ways that are healthy and supportive; ways that dissolve separation and return you home to Love.

Agitation is the energy surfacing through a small opening, but it has not yet expanded into the level of consciousness needed for its healing.

Resentment closes the heart, blocking the higher awareness of love that is necessary to transform the situation.

Go beyond the level of consciousness that created this painful experience for you.

Acknowledge and feel the pain beneath the resentment.

Practice compassion for yourself, and when you are ready, for the other person as well.

Allow yourself to be guided towards the next aligned action.

It may be a conversation, setting a boundary, making a decision, forgiveness, or something else entirely.

What matters is that you allow the energy to move.

Prayer is an especially supportive tool to work through resentment.

Praying for the person whom you feel resentment towards can help to relieve you of it.

Pray each day for their peace, healing, or all that Love desires for them.

Pray, even if you do not yet mean it, for your prayers will support the pain in healing and eventually the words will become wholly true.

When you consciously work towards healing resentment, you dissolve and release the burdens you carry.

You go beyond the illusion and separation of the thinking mind and ground into ultimate truth.

When you consciously work towards healing resentment, you allow love to lead you home.

TREAT YOURSELF
WITH COMPASSION

"The first step in spiritual life is to have compassion. A person who is kind and loving never needs to go searching for God. God rushes toward any heart that beats with compassion-it is God's favorite place."
—Amma

YOU TOOK this birth to evolve, which means that making mistakes is a natural part of the path of growth.

Mistakes are an essential aspect of how we as humans learn. This is part of the experience of being in a body.

Knowing this, it is necessary to practice self-compassion when mistakes are made.

Self-compassion means speaking to and treating yourself the way you would a small child or beloved animal.

It means treating yourself with gentleness, kindness, and love.

The ego often carries the belief that being hard on yourself will lead to the growth you desire, but this has been disproven time and time again.

What is true is that self-compassion is motivating, supportive, and empowering.

When you treat yourself with compassion, you are better able to navigate challenges, perform your duties, and make lasting, meaningful changes.

When your ego tells you stories of unworthiness and shame, self-compassion helps you speak gently to yourself, as you bathe yourself in love and understanding.

Mistakes are opportunities to practice accepting yourself in all your humanness.

Mistakes are opportunities to practice embracing yourself in compassion.

Self-compassion invites you to remember that ultimately everything will be okay.

Rather than berating or shaming yourself, you align with love and move through the challenge with greater ease and trust.

Speaking kindly to yourself and practicing compassion during times of challenge or stress improves every situation and supports you in navigating life with greater acceptance and surrender.

When you treat yourself with care, you are more able to extend that same care to others.

When you treat yourself with love, you are more able to extend that love to others.

Self-compassion strengthens not only the relationship you have with yourself, but the relationships you have with others, as well.

It nurtures self-acceptance and allows you to be more accepting and forgiving with others.

The more you treat yourself with compassion, the less you feel the need to displace your own pain onto others.

The more you are kind to yourself, the less your ego needs to think or act in ways that harm others.

When you make a mistake, you are being guided to deepen your compassion for yourself and your fellow neighbors in existence.

When you practice compassion with yourself, as well as plants, animals, and all beings, you live in alignment with love.

You live in alignment with that which created you and that which you are created of.

When you practice compassion with self and others, you purify your entire being.

Self-compassion supports you in opening your heart and feeling more love in daily life. It creates space for greater presence, service, creativity, and connection.

Self-compassion is a gift you give not only to yourself, but to others as well.

It allows you to treat yourself in accordance with your true nature.

It is how the Divine desires you to care for yourself.

When you practice self-compassion, you bring peace to your heart.

Peace in the world begins with peace in our hearts.

When you practice self-compassion, you allow yourself to be guided by your deepest being.

You become a vessel for the Love that you are and the love that desires to be expressed through you.

When you practice self-compassion, you support all of existence in returning home to Love.

FORGIVENESS IS THE WAY TO PEACE AND FREEDOM

"For when forgiveness has purified the mind and the heart and the emotional field of your own being, you will discover that you exist only to extend Love." —The Way of the Heart

CERTAIN SPIRITUAL TEXTS emphasize forgiveness as the foundation of healing.

Once you begin to understand the sheer power of forgiveness, it becomes clear why its importance is so heavily emphasized.

The more you learn about forgiveness, the more you understand why some texts focus deeply on what forgiveness is, how to practice it, and the miracles it offers.

Forgiveness is an essential aspect of living a healthy life grounded in truth and love.

Forgiveness allows you to remember the truth that we are all creations of the Divine, each an extension of God's love. This remembrance helps you to release illusion and ground into the knowing of your oneness with all beings.

For many, forgiveness is a foreign concept because it is often not taught, understood, or prioritized in our world today.

A Course in Miracles teaches that a miracle is a shift in perception from fear to love, and forgiveness is presented as a fundamental shift in perception.

So, forgiveness itself is a miracle.

Judgments and grievances are rooted in the mind, the ego. They stem from separation and fear, creating anger, resentment, and guilt. True forgiveness allows us to see beyond ego-level actions and recognize the underlying innocence and divine nature of every soul.

Forgiveness does not condone or excuse harmful behavior. Rather, it recognizes that all hurtful actions are ultimately cries for help and healing.

Forgiveness is not just about letting go of past hurts. It is a shift in consciousness that transforms your understanding of yourself and others.

It is a new way of seeing the world, looking upon oneself and others through the eyes of the Beloved, recognizing the innocence of the soul behind the humanness, understanding our deep interconnectedness, and knowing that any hurtful behavior is a cry for love.

Forgiveness sees through the illusion of separation and recognizes the eternal truth that we are all one.

Through forgiveness, you transcend the ego's judgments and align with a higher perspective that reflects the unconditional love of the Divine.

Forgiveness is truly a gift you give to yourself, and not just another.

It cultivates healing, peace, and a deeper connection to your truest being.

Some sacred texts describe forgiveness as the act of releasing false perceptions that you project onto others.

You project onto others that which you deny in yourself, as a way to rid yourself of the personal attributes you reject and disown.

It is a way of saying, "Here, I don't want this. This is bad or makes me unlovable, so I'll put it on you instead."

The opposite of forgiveness is judgment.

Judgement creates separation and guilt, both for the one being judged and the one doing the judging. This is why you may feel guilt or shame after engaging in gossip.

Humans often judge themselves harshly. Self-condemnation creates feelings of separation and guilt, making self-forgiveness just as essential as forgiving others.

When you judge, blame, or condemn yourself, it is a sacred call to forgive oneself.

When you or another do something hurtful, it is always a cry for help and healing.

You are not bad. The other person is not bad.

In fact, the practice of forgiveness always includes forgiving yourself. You are either forgiving yourself for judging yourself and not seeing the truth and innocence of your soul, or you are forgiving yourself for projecting false judgments onto another and not seeing them in the truth of their being.

The more you practice forgiving yourself, the more you will be able to forgive others.

Forgiveness is not something you do just once.

Forgiveness is a practice.

It is something you learn, something you cultivate, and something that becomes easier over time.

That being said, you cannot skip straight to forgiveness when there is pain that must be acknowledged.

You cannot bypass your feelings and jump directly to forgiveness, as this suppresses life force energy within you that longs to be honored and felt.

The way out is through.

Acknowledging and feeling your emotions is part of the pathway to forgiveness. Without this step, you cannot truly forgive.

Allow the grief and rage to exist. Allow the fear and distrust to arise. Allow the pain that is within you to be.

Feelings want to be felt. It is essential to give them space to arise, abide, and move through you.

Walk the middle path; you do not want to become trapped in pain and hurt forever, as doing so will halt your evolution, nor do you want to practice forgiveness before you feel ready.

You do not need to be with someone physically to forgive them or ask for their forgiveness. The person does not even need to be alive.

In this quantum universe, you can connect with any soul regarding forgiveness.

The one you most need to forgive may be yourself, another, or God.

Forgiveness is a practice you learn, deepen, and refine over time.

Feeling and forgiving do not follow a perfectly linear path, where you feel your feelings first and forgive afterwards.

You may oscillate between the two, but over time, compassion, understanding, and forgiveness will become your primary experience.

Forgiveness begins with yourself and then extends outwards to others.

Though in truth, there are no "others," for we are all one.

Forgiveness allows you to see yourself and others as creations of the Divine.

Forgiveness returns you to the truth that we are brothers, sisters, and neighbors in existence, and that there is no energy you can be aware of in another that you do not also have within yourself.

Forgiveness is the knowing that at the core of every being is Love.

It is a practice, and it may take time to feel fully grounded in a space of forgiveness.

That is okay. Be patient with yourself and trust this holy process.

Peace and freedom come by the grace of God and arrive when they are meant to.

The pathway to forgiveness looks different for everyone, but there are things that can deepen your practice, such as acceptance of the situation, feeling your feelings, and prayer.

Accept where you are on your journey. Do not rush your process.

Allow yourself to be exactly where you are.

Trust your path of healing, and allow yourself the time you need to feel the feelings present for you regarding this person or situation.

When you are deep in the pain, the pain must be processed first.

Do not pressure or guilt yourself into forgiveness before you feel ready. Doing so will only stifle your process.

Prayer is a powerful tool here.

Pray on it.

Pray and ask for help to feel everything that stands in the way of your forgiveness.

Pray for help to forgive.

Ask for help to see yourself or another in truth and through the eyes of Love.

You can write a forgiveness prayer that you recite daily, asking for that which your heart yearns for.

Pray for the one you want to forgive.

Pray to be able to forgive.

Forgiving others becomes easier the more you learn to accept and love yourself.

Forgiving others becomes easier the more you are able to forgive yourself for all of your humanness.

Taking any of these actions will powerfully support your practice of forgiveness, but forgiveness itself is given by God's grace.

It arrives in alignment with divine timing.

When you forgive, you see clearly.

When you forgive, you see Love.

Forgiveness supports you in liberating your mind from the illusion of separation.

It guides your heart back to true peace.

Forgiveness returns you to the love that you are and the love at the center of all of existence.

PURIFICATION RETURNS
YOU TO YOUR TRUE NATURE

*"If a mirror is covered with dirt, it won't reflect one's face. A man
cannot realize his true Self unless his heart is pure."*
—Ramakrishna

PURIFICATION IS the process of releasing the illusions of the ego
and returning home to the Love that you are.

To purify means to cleanse yourself of everything that is not love.

To rid yourself of the thoughts, feelings, and attachments that are
born of fear and separation.

Purification is essential for humans, as the ego is often lost in
illusion.

Returning home to Love involves realizing your true Self,
returning to your truest nature, and desiring only God.

Returning home to Love allows you to surrender to the Beloved.

Purification assists you in releasing all that is not truth and love
within you.

Purification is a practice you engage in regularly, as part of your daily life.

Practices that support purification include prayer, meditation, chanting, mantra, truth-telling, feeling your emotions, taking responsibility for your actions, service, devotion, and any other practice that leads you back to the light of the universe and the holiness of your heart.

Communicating truthfully and respectfully is an act of purification.

Aligning your words and actions with love is an act of purification.

Serving others is an act of purification.

When you offer your actions to the Divine and release all attachment to the results, you are purified.

Serving others purifies you.

Repeating the Divine Name purifies you.

Suffering throws you into the holy fire of purification.

Actions rooted in your soul's purpose purify you.

Devotion to love is a sacred act of purification.

Purification requires the acknowledgment of the ego-based aspects of yourself that are rooted in fear and separation. In order to purify, these parts of yourself must be brought into the light of awareness.

Purification is a continuous practice that supports you in releasing the agonizing burdens of the ego.

When you purify, you let go of that which you no longer want to carry and that which no longer serves you.

When you purify, you release illusion from your mind, body, and spirit.

You clear away heaviness and create space for greater peace, freedom, and joy.

Purification is any practice that returns you home to Love.

Practices that support your purification help you to become a more compassionate human and deepen the love in your heart.

Purification opens you to miracles and expands your awareness of the Love within and all around you.

Purification supports you in embodying clearer vision, vision that sees only Love.

THE EGO SPEAKS FIRST,
THE SOUL SPEAKS SECOND

"Take no notice of the ego and its activities, but see only the light behind." —Ramana Maharshi

THOUGHTS ARE NOT FACTS.

Simply because you think something, that does not make it true.

The ego speaks first, the soul speaks second.

Or rather, the whispers of the soul, ever-abiding as they are, often require stillness and presence to be heard.

More often than not, the ego makes itself known first through thoughts of judgment, criticism, and fear.

There are moments when the soul whispers first, and the ego immediately attempts to override it, again, always out of fear.

The focus here, however, is on the commonplace thoughts of the mind that arise and fade all throughout the day. The initial thoughts of the ego that surface when your inner voice is filled with critique, self-righteousness, or superiority.

The thoughts that arise as soon as your awareness settles on a person, place, or thing. Thoughts of jealousy, comparison, or greed; violence, objectification, or attack.

It is the nature of the mind for thoughts to continuously arise and fade all throughout the day.

Your thoughts are not who you are.

Your thoughts do not reflect your true being.

Only loving thoughts are true.

Sometimes thoughts may arise that disappoint, shock, or frighten you. These thoughts are not rooted in truth and do not reflect your true being. They are born of separation and are rooted in fear.

When you give yourself a moment of presence and silence to go beyond the surface thoughts of the mind, you are able to tune into the radiant, loving whispers of the soul.

You cannot stop thoughts from arising, but you can decide whether or not to identify with them.

You can choose whether or not to listen to them.

You can choose to ignore thoughts rooted in fear and be guided only by those rooted in truth.

You can choose to allow only loving thoughts to lead you.

Thoughts come and go, but they are not who you are.

You are something far greater, more expansive, and vast.

You are a creation of the Divine's love, holiness, and glory.

You are infinite, you are sacred.

If an unloving thought arises in your awareness, it is untrue.

Whether you acknowledge it, engage with it, believe it, or allow it to guide you is your choice.

Thoughts arise and thoughts fade away.

There is no need to identify with your thoughts; they are merely like clouds passing through the sky.

Your thoughts are not who you are, they are not your true nature, and they do not reflect upon your truest self.

Unloving thoughts do not reflect your goodness or worth.

Judgmental thoughts about yourself or others are attack thoughts of the ego. They are rooted in separation.

The ego speaks first, the soul speaks second.

Fear makes itself known first, and then you can consciously choose to turn your being towards love.

The ego is relentless, yet truth is always available just a step beyond the noise.

Sometimes it can feel very difficult to know which voice is speaking or which voice is true.

Let that be okay.

Offer any confusion to the Divine and ask for the answer to be revealed. Trust the answer will become clear when it is meant to.

You are not your thoughts.

You are that which observes them.

Sometimes it is necessary to allow feelings within to move through you before you can access your inner truth.

When an unloving thought arises, remind yourself, it is simply the ego speaking, and the ego is rooted in fear. Pause, breathe, give yourself a moment, and allow your soul to speak next.

The ego speaks loudly, urgently, and fearfully. It speaks with criticism, lack, and separation.

Your soul speaks with infinite trust and eternal love.

Go beyond the insanity of the mind and tune into the subtle, truthful whispers of your soul.

Practice noticing when the fear of the ego is speaking and when love is leading the way.

Practice discernment, not judgment.

Discerning what is safe and aligned for you is important.

When you think, speak, and act in alignment with love, you feel connected to your true nature.

You feel open, grounded, and expanded.

You feel connected to truth and your deepest being.

When you act out of alignment with love, you are left feeling guilt, sorrow, and despair.

You are not your mind.

You are not your thoughts.

You are the light of consciousness behind them.

Your soul's voice is rooted in truth, compassion, and wisdom.

Your soul always speaks with love, no matter what it is addressing.

Your soul is your true self—the eternal, blissful core of who you are, unattached to form, labels, and identity.

Your soul is the part of you that has never forgotten it is pure, boundless, and eternal love.

Your soul knows it is one with all, always.

Your soul is love and is devoted to love.

Your soul is the truth of who you are.

You are the abode of Love.

YOUR EXTERNAL WORLD
REFLECTS YOUR INTERNAL WORLD

"Let me look on the world I see as the representation of my own state of mind." —A Course in Miracles

LIFE IS AN INSIDE JOB.

Your external world reflects your internal world.

What is outside of you reflects what is within you back to you.

What is outside of you reflects the lessons, needs, and desires of your soul back to you through other people, relational dynamics, challenges, and the happenings of your daily life.

Life is constantly inviting you into your next layer of evolution.

If you desire to change an external situation in your life, you must change how you perceive and interact with that situation internally, as well.

What are your thoughts, feelings, and beliefs about the situation?

What limits are present in your thinking about it?

What assumptions, agreements, or illusions do you hold that no longer serve you?

What stories about yourself, your life, and the world continuously loop on repeat in your mind?

When you truly change your beliefs, you change your life.

Life is an inside job.

Consider what the experiences you navigate are reflecting back to you and what they are attempting to support you with.

How is a certain experience attempting to support your healing and evolution?

There is a purpose for this particular situation arising in your reality.

This circumstance has arrived with profound potential to help you heal and grow.

If you want to change how someone responds and relates to you, change how you respond and relate to them.

If you desire honesty, be honest.

If you desire peace, be peaceful.

If you desire kindness, be kind.

Your experience of reality includes the projection of your thoughts, beliefs, agreements, stories, and perceptions.

Your world is created by and reflecting back to you the universe of your mind.

Your daily life is built upon your past karmas, the lessons you need to learn, and God's grace.

Your reality is masterfully designed to help you heal and evolve in the exact ways you took this birth to.

It mirrors parts of yourself back to you that you have rejected or disowned.

This is why, for example, someone who suppresses their anger may encounter people who are full of anger in their external reality. Their outer world is encouraging them to acknowledge, feel, and express their own anger in healthy ways. They are being invited into their truth, voice, and authentic expression.

What about you is being reflected back to you through the situations in your life?

What within you is asking for your attention in order to shift the world around you?

What is unresolved within you is always seeking resolution.

Because this is an infinitely loving universe, everything arises to support your evolution.

Spirit and soul, both one and the same, are the most magnificent and miraculous poets. Your daily life is surrounded by and completely immersed in sacred symbolism—not only in your wisdom-filled dreams, but in the experiences of your waking life, as well.

Meaning surrounds you.

Your car breaks down. Where in life do you feel stuck, or are you having trouble moving forward?

Your sink is clogged. Where might feelings be suppressed or emotions feel stuck?

A beloved pet is experiencing a physical symptom. How might this symptom be reflecting a conflict in your own life?

The circumstances of your life exist with purpose and meaning.

When you begin to decode the messages of your dreams and

waking life, you begin connecting with yourself and the Divine on ever-deepening levels.

Your reality is always guiding you home towards acceptance, truth, and love.

When something challenging, triggering, or confusing arises, pause.

Breathe.

Make space to acknowledge and feel any feelings present.

When you are ready, reflect on why this situation is arising in your life.

How is this experience meant to support your healing?

What is this situation attempting to assist you with?

What is this circumstance reflecting back to you?

Tune into what is being communicated to you.

When you focus your awareness on the meaning within a situation, you are able to use the happenings of daily life to support the evolution of your soul.

Your external world is reflecting your inner world back to you.

Allow yourself to see and receive its messages.

When you tend to the universe within with loving awareness, you change the world around you.

When you desire to see truth and love, your reality will support you in doing just that.

You may not receive the experiences your mind desires along the way, but you can be certain you will receive the experiences you need.

Become aware of where your focus lies.

Reflect on what you are projecting outwards.

Reflect on where your beliefs are creating your reality.

The garden within you thrives when you attune to, honor, and nurture it.

Such loving cultivation will be reflected in all that surrounds you.

NOTHING OUTSIDE
YOU CAN SAVE YOU

"Happiness is your nature. It is not wrong to desire it. What is wrong is seeking it outside when it is inside."
—Ramana Maharshi

NOTHING CAN WHOLLY, eternally, or completely fulfill you except for the love of God.

Nothing can ultimately satisfy you except for Divine Love.

No dream realized or desire obtained can ever bring lasting joy, because nothing outside of you can stop the universal longing within to realize your Self and awaken to your true nature.

No gratification is wholly fulfilling, leaving you without wanting more, except the desire to return to that from which you came.

The desire to reunite with the Beloved.

Everything in life is transient; everything in this world is changing.

The only thing that never changes or disappears is the love of God.

This does not mean to ignore your dreams or desires, as they are essential to your evolution and the offering of your open heart to the world.

But it is vital to understand that nothing outside of you can complete you.

You are an aspect of the One that has taken a human body and incarnation. You have been sent on a journey to remember all that you forgot.

Fulfillment comes from within.

Peace comes from within.

No one can save you and no one can make you whole.

No amount of achievement or success can heal what yearns to be healed within you.

No one can prevent your soul's longing to embark and continue upon its evolutionary journey home to Love.

Your soul desires ultimate truth.

Your soul desires unity and love.

Nothing outside of you can fulfill you because you seek to remember that which you truly are.

You seek to reunite with that which created you.

You are on a quest to remember your miraculous and holy nature.

You are on a quest to remember unconditional love.

When you are devoted to Love, every aspect of your life benefits.

No matter what you are called to navigate, you walk with trust and faith.

When you desire only Love, you know true freedom.

When you desire only Love, you find true peace.

WHAT YOU GIVE, YOU RECEIVE

"Karma is the law that works for righteousness; it is the healing hand of God." —Nisargadatta Maharaj

WHAT YOU OFFER to the world, you receive in return.

You may receive it quickly, or it may take lifetimes.

There is a law of karma in this universe.

It is not a law of punishment, but a law of balance and equality.

A law that ensures you are always guided back to Love.

Because this is a loving universe, all karma is designed to support your healing.

To assist you in evolving in the exact ways your soul desires.

Are you offering hurt or are you offering love?

Are you treating yourself and others respectfully or with disregard?

Are you reacting from ego or responding from your heart?

Your life continuously presents you with the precise circumstances needed to support you in healing in the ways you took this birth to heal.

When you hurt another, the universe aims to help you understand what that hurt feels like, so you can be more loving in the future.

When you selflessly give to another, you receive that love in return.

When you judge, manipulate, or attack another, you send out energy you would not wish to receive.

When you serve another, no matter how small, you receive that loving kindness back to you.

Are you treating others the way you wish to be treated?

Do you want to receive what you are offering to the world?

The more you move through life connected to the center of your being, the less hurtful karma you create for yourself.

When you move throughout the world humbly rooted in love, you allow yourself to be an instrument of the Divine.

Your life is past karmas playing out.

Through intention and action, you are constantly designing your future circumstances.

Painful karma is never meant to punish you, only heal you.

Suffering exists with the sole purpose of leading you towards the eternal, that which offers supreme peace, absolute truth, and infinite love.

The ultimate purpose of karma is to guide the soul towards the realization of the Self and to lead in the direction of liberation and awakening.

To help you open your heart, be humble, and see the One in all.

Life after life, through suffering and joy, you are continuously being carried closer and closer back home to Love.

May you begin to notice the spaces where it feels challenging to act with love, as noticing is a crucial step on the path of healing.

May you reflect on why it feels difficult, and be supported in healing these hurts.

How can you offer more love to this world, both for yourself and others?

How can you support yourself in being loving awareness—to see yourself and others as souls, with the knowing that we are all one —and responding from that space?

May your life be an expression of love.

May your life offer love to this world.

May your life leave this world with more love than when you found it.

A life of love is a life of prayer.

A life of love is a life of purpose.

A life filled with love is a life well lived.

Offering love to the world begins with offering love to yourself.

What you give originates within you.

When you accept and forgive yourself, you more easily accept and forgive others.

When you love yourself, everything you give is rooted in that love.

When you honor the miracle of your being, you honor the miracle of all beings.

So ask yourself, do you want to receive what you are offering?

Let love be your guide, one moment at a time.

Love knows the way back home.

SUFFERING IS UNIVERSAL

"Suffering is the sandpaper of our incarnation. It does its work of shaping us." —Ram Dass

SUFFERING IS UNIVERSAL.

You are not alone in experiencing pain, even when your mind attempts to convince you otherwise.

All people experience hardship, and while the form and degree of difficulty vary, each is relative to the one who experiences it.

We took these births to evolve, and the challenges we must go through are designed to support us in doing just that.

Saints and sages teach that suffering is God's grace, a gift from God itself, because it can bring you into ever-deepening levels of truth, wisdom, and compassion.

It can lead you into union with the Divine.

Suffering has the power to awaken profound healing and spiritual evolution.

It can bring you to that which is eternal and support you in surrendering, opening your heart, and deepening your connection with Divine Love.

Your mind may question why your life is so difficult when others seem to have it so easy. It may tell you that you are less worthy than others because of the challenges you face.

These are mere stories of the mind and not thoughts rooted in truth.

We are often unaware of the depth of pain and struggle that exists in others.

You are not alone in your pain.

Navigating hardship does not have any reflection upon your worth.

Encountering challenges is part of the human experience.

You are brave when you face and move through these challenges.

Accepting the opportunity to evolve is a sheer act of courage.

The particular challenges you face in this incarnation are divinely designed to support you in healing and evolving in the exact ways your soul desires.

Whether physical, mental, emotional, or spiritual, these challenges exist with great purpose.

There is not one hardship that arises in your life without the purpose of helping you grow.

Challenges support the ego in letting go.

Challenges support the ego in opening to Love.

When hardship is faced and navigated, you gain a deeper awareness of your abilities and strength.

You gain the knowing that you can do hard things.

You become more aware of your fortitude, maturity, and ability to face challenges.

Your compassion deepens.

You awaken to what is possible when you allow yourself to be guided by Love, even in, and especially in, the most challenging and painful of circumstances.

You cannot control the curriculum you navigate in this lifetime, but you can choose whether you resist or cooperate with the evolution at hand.

You can decide whether or not you will use your life as a vehicle for the evolution of your soul.

Sometimes we do not allow challenges to serve their true purpose in bringing us closer to the Divine.

Resistance is always an option, and it is very often part of the path of evolution.

There will be times when resisting what you feel is best for you does not feel like a choice at all. Moments when you know which path is most aligned, but do not yet feel strong enough to move in that direction.

Other times you may find yourself swinging back and forth between resistance and cooperation, which is perfectly natural.

Resisting does not at all make you bad, merely human. Yet it can be quite painful, keeping you from spaces of deeper peace, alignment, and love.

And sometimes, that very resistance creates the necessary suffering that becomes the catalyst for profound healing and transformation in your life.

Growth is often two steps forward and one step back.

Growth is a spiral.

You will be asked to revisit similar themes and lessons throughout your lifetime, on ever-deepening levels.

You are not alone in being asked to face challenges, nor are you alone in navigating them.

You were never alone.

You will never be alone.

Everyone's journey is different, and you are exactly where you are supposed to be at this moment in time to heal and grow in the precise ways your soul desires.

Love is holding you, Love is guiding you, and Love is leading you home.

ANY ENERGY YOU CAN BE AWARE OF IN ANOTHER ALSO EXISTS WITHIN YOU

"Who then is less than you? Who then is worthy of your judgment? No one. Who then is equal to you? Everyone. And who then is worthy of your love? Everyone." —The Way of the Heart

WHEN YOU CRITICIZE or condemn another, you project aspects of yourself outward.

You take the parts of yourself that you do not yet accept or love, or the parts in need of healing, and you place them onto another.

We are all connected, which means there is no energy in another that is not also within you.

The intensity of that energy and the way in which it manifests may be different, but it is not something that belongs solely to another.

There is no one who is less than you.

There is no one who is better than you.

The true nature of every being is Divine Love.

We are each at different places upon our path, but the destination remains the same for us all.

When someone activates pain within you, a sacred opportunity for healing arises.

There is something within this person that touches upon a part of yourself you have not yet loved.

Triggers are signals pointing to spaces within that are yearning for your love.

The pain that others trigger in you is already within you. The trigger simply brings it to the surface, into the light of awareness, where it can be acknowledged, felt, and healed.

When you notice you are judging someone or feeling triggered by someone, be present with the feelings that surface within you.

Notice, name, and feel them.

Allow the feelings to move through you.

When you are ready, reflect on why this particular person, trait, or action triggered you.

What about them touched on something painful within you?

Explore, discover, and accept.

When you feel critical of or triggered by another, a holy opportunity arises to turn your focus inward and be present with what is truly wanting your attention.

Every moment of your life is an opportunity to evolve.

To heal through your thoughts, beliefs, and actions.

To return home to Love in each moment of your life.

This return is the ultimate desire of the soul.

Your life is the vehicle through which it is fulfilled.

Practice accepting the parts of others that remind you of the unloved parts of yourself.

Practice loving yourself and others, because it is truly all the same in the end.

THOSE WHO HURT
OTHERS ARE HURTING

*"One works on oneself as a gift to other people so that one doesn't create
more suffering."* —*Ram Dass*

THOSE WHO HURT others are hurting.

Pain is a call home to truth, a call home to Love.

When you hurt another, you are in pain.

When pain is not acknowledged, processed, and felt, it can affect
others.

One who is suffering may unconsciously project their pain onto
others because they are unable to carry the burden themselves.

While this may briefly relieve their ego of suffering, it ultimately
creates more pain, in the form of guilt, shame, or self-
righteousness.

When someone hurts another, deep down, it is a cry for help and
healing.

If you find yourself being hurtful towards another, whether internally or externally, recognize that you yourself are hurting.

This is not about the other person; it is about you. They are activating pain within you that is yearning to be felt.

Acknowledging when this occurs is an essential and beautiful step in healing and repairing the hurt. Offer what happened to the Divine. Ask for help. Allow yourself to receive the support you are worthy of.

Ask to be released from fear and separation and returned to truth and love.

When you hurt someone, an opportunity arises to take responsibility for your actions, repair the situation, and learn from the experience.

When you hurt another, a grand opportunity arises to practice self-compassion and self-love.

When you are hurt by another, an opportunity arises to feel your feelings, resolve the conflict, and practice understanding.

When someone hurts you, a sacred opportunity arises to practice forgiveness.

Pain is caused by the ego, and pain arises within the ego.

The purpose of pain is to bring you to that which is eternal and lead you to that which brings true peace.

Pain exists to help you open your heart and return to truth and love.

Pain is not the truth of who you are.

When met with tenderness, sorrow becomes a doorway back to your infinite, loving, and luminous Self.

Be patient with yourself and others as wounds are navigated.

Pain is a pathway to surrender.

Surrender is a pathway to trust.

Trust is a pathway to devotion.

Devotion is a pathway to an open heart.

Pain is a pathway home to Love.

Peace in the world begins with peace in your heart.

HARDSHIP IS DESIGNED TO SUPPORT YOUR EVOLUTION

"It can be painful, but the bliss of getting free is very great, too."
—Ram Dass

EVERYTHING THAT ARISES in your reality exists to support your healing, growth, and return home to Love.

When a challenge arises in your life, it is always with great purpose.

It is never random and never meaningless.

Sometimes we recognize how certain hardships have supported us only after the experience is over.

The ego, however, often resists the process while the hardship is occurring.

Challenges are an inherent part of the human experience.

All beings experience pain.

Anandamayi Ma taught that painful worldly circumstances have the power to initiate us onto a path of seeking the Divine, ultimately aligning us more deeply with love and a greater experience of true peace. She called such experiences "an expression of His Mercy."

An expression of the Divine's love.

This does not at all remove the immense pain that can be present while navigating difficulties, but offers a thread of purpose or meaning to situations that can appear to have absolutely none.

Every challenge is designed to support your healing and evolution.

When a challenge arises, instead of resisting, practice being present with what is.

Meet the challenge in the present moment.

Acknowledge any feelings within you.

Allow your emotions to move through you.

Ask for support.

Engage in practices that assist you in navigating the challenge.

Allow the pain to break your heart open and transform you from the inside out.

Let go of the parts of yourself that must die through the process.

Give yourself the time and space you need to process the experience before seeking deeper meaning. This may be moments, months, or years.

When you are ready, reflect on how this challenge is meant to support you.

Why has this particular challenge appeared in your life?

How is it designed to assist you with your evolution?

Reflect on what it may be here to help you with.

Is it guiding you to release attachment, feel your feelings, speak up, or trust yourself?

Is it leading you to open your heart, set a boundary, stay present, or surrender to the Divine?

Perhaps it is pushing you onto a path of greater alignment, to live your dharma, or to heal pain within that is yearning to be set free.

Remember, this challenge is precisely placed in your life at this very moment in time to help you heal, grow, and return home to Love.

Your ego may resist this truth; that is natural.

This experience is designed to serve your highest good.

You can use this experience to ground deeper into truth and love.

Offer any questions, resistance, or doubts to the Divine.

Pray on it.

The answers will come when they are meant to.

More will be revealed in divine timing.

You are exactly where you are supposed to be.

Allow this pain, moment by moment, to wear away the illusions of the ego and lead you to that which is beyond all suffering.

Allow it to lead you to your true Self, which remains unaltered by the happenings of your life.

The part of you that is Love, has always been Love, and will forever be only Love.

The part of you that divinely trusts and surrenders with pure devotion to the present moment.

Allow the pain of your life to bring you to your knees.

Sincerely offer your entire being to Love.

You are infinitely held, cared for, and supported.

Divine guidance is available for you in every moment.

You are exactly where you are supposed to be.

REJECTION IS A BLESSING IN DISGUISE

"Have complete trust in Him in spite of everything."
—Anandamayi Ma

WHEN A DOOR CLOSES in your life, especially one that you longed for or expected to remain open, pain can arise.

The mind may tell you stories of comparison and unworthiness, attempting to explain why you feel abandoned by the universe.

These are stories of illusion. These are stories disconnected from truth.

This pathway did not open for you because it was never meant to.

Rejection is Divine orchestration at work.

Rejection is the universe conspiring in your favor.

Rejection is part of the perfection of the Divine's plan.

The master plan at play always exists for your highest and greatest good.

The happenings of your life exist to support your deepest healing and most expanded evolution.

If that person never rejected you, you would have never been guided to the person you love today.

If that job opportunity had not resulted in a no, you would never have gone through the dark night that propelled you onto a path of healing.

If that attractive but misaligned living situation had chosen you, you would never have been guided to the nourishing and aligned spaces truly meant for you.

Sometimes you are able to see in hindsight how rejection was, in fact, God's grace at play all along.

The ego can have trouble trusting this in the moment, as it may feed you thoughts of fear and separation.

It may tell you stories of how opportunities arise for others, but not for you.

The truth is that rejection arises because it is the most supportive experience for you to undergo at that moment in time.

Perhaps the rejection will lead you to deep healing, an opportunity of greater alignment, or a brand new path you did not know existed.

A closed door can lead to great healing.

A closed door can lead to exponential evolution.

The Beloved knows best and infinitely better than any ego.

A door may not have opened because the opportunity was not as aligned as your mind believed it to be.

A door may not have opened in order to lead you to the divine dharma of your incarnation.

Rejection is the universe protecting you.

Rejection is the universe supporting you.

Rejection is divine redirection.

What appears to be rejection is actually Supreme Love leading you exactly where you are meant to be.

Rejection can guide you towards a path of true alignment.

Rejection can lead you to choose yourself.

Rejection can return you home to Love.

Sometimes, it is in not getting what you want that the greatest healing unfolds.

The ego wants what it wants and it wants it now, but God always knows what is truly best for you.

Everything that happens in your life is for your highest and greatest good, in support of your soul's deepest evolution.

You took this birth to evolve, and that is what the experiences of your life are constantly assisting you with.

When a door closes that you wished had opened, let yourself be present with the pain it brings.

Let your heart break.

The pain is asking to be felt.

This pain is present to guide you inward, into spaces that are yearning for your attention and love.

This pain is present to lead you to trust, faith, and the Divine.

Feel your feelings, receive support, and know that you are being carried exactly where you are meant to be.

Tend to your heart.

Trust the mystery.

More will be revealed in time.

This challenge is helping to mold you into the person you need to become in order to live the life you incarnated for.

There is immense purpose in this experience, and it is never ever to punish you.

It is only to assist you.

You are being protected, redirected, or guided elsewhere, to where you truly long to be.

When one door closes, another will open; one of even greater alignment, in divine timing.

You are exactly where you are supposed to be in order to heal and grow in the precise ways your soul desires.

LESSONS CONTINUE TO REPEAT AND GROW LOUDER UNTIL THEY ARE LEARNED

"We have to allow the power that we don't understand to take care of us. This mysterious power knows what your needs are."
—Robert Adams

LESSONS CONTINUE to repeat and grow louder until they are learned.

This is not to punish you, hurt you, or drive you mad, but rather to encourage you to evolve in the ways your soul desires.

To support you in embarking upon the sacred healing journey you took this birth for.

To help you realize the "why" of your sacred incarnation.

When the ego continues to resist your soul's evolution and the lessons life presents, the messages grow louder in order to get your attention.

The more you resist evolution, the more life will bring forth challenges of growing discomfort, until the healing your soul desires can no longer be ignored.

This is a law of love, though it seldom feels that way.

Even when a lesson has your attention, your ego may still resist it. This is natural.

Again, the messages will continue to grow in intensity over time, persistently inviting you to align with your soul's longing to heal and grow.

This is not cruelty.

This is love.

This is how a loving universe supports your return to truth and your true nature.

Resistance amplifies pain over time.

And yet, it can also help spark the very suffering needed to guide you towards the healing your soul deeply desires.

Resistance is always of the ego and never of the soul.

The ego fears evolution while the soul longs for it, for the soul knows the magnificence to which it leads.

In an infinitely loving universe, anything standing in the way of love must be brought into the light of awareness to be seen and healed.

Sometimes the messages arrive as small discomforts.

Other times, they may arrive in the form of a crisis.

Whatever their form, they always come with an invitation to heal and grow.

When you cooperate with the evolution your soul desires, you evolve in real time.

You initiate evolution in action.

This is universal law.

Everything in this universe exists to return you home to Love.

You came here to evolve, to dissolve the illusion of separateness, and to return to ultimate truth.

You came here to remember the holiness of your being, embody the divine light within, and reunite with the boundless radiance that you are.

Anything standing in the way must rise to the surface to be healed.

In the hero's journey of your life, certain themes, messages, and archetypal experiences will repeat themselves. These are the precise lessons you are navigating and learning through this incarnation.

Growth is not linear; it is a spiral.

Healing unfolds in cycles.

You take two steps forward, one step back, and two steps forward once again.

Each time, meeting similar themes at deeper and deeper levels.

When you are being guided to grow in a specific way, the message will continue growing louder until the lesson is learned.

As awful and uncomfortable as this can sometimes feel, this is the universe's way of continuously supporting your highest and greatest good.

If everything exists to return you home to Love, then every circumstance in your life is here to support that holy return.

To help you live as your most authentic and empowered self.

To help you love yourself and others.

To help you align with your soul's truest desires.

What is rooted in illusion longs to be healed.

What is rooted in love longs to be shared and celebrated.

Trust where you are being guided, even when your mind may intensely resist.

You can trust the Divine to support you every step along the way.

You can trust the Divine to carry you exactly where you are meant to be.

You can trust that every aspect of your life is designed to guide you home.

FIND A PRACTICE THAT SUPPORTS YOU IN RETURNING HOME TO LOVE

"How many lives are frittered away, age after age, in endless coming and going. Find out who you are!" —Anandamayi Ma

IT IS essential on the path of healing and evolution to have practices that resonate for you and support you in returning home to Love.

Practice supports you with presence.

Practice helps you hear truth.

Practice allows you to remember.

Examples of practice include prayer, meditation, japa (repetition of the Divine Name), chanting, asana, dance, journaling, breathwork, playing an instrument, and creating art.

It is the nature of the human mind to distract, disconnect, and believe in the illusion of separation over and over again. This is why it is imperative to have aligned practices that return you home to truth and Love, over and over again.

Your practice is there for you whether you feel wonderful or awful, joyful or full of grief.

A practice is not something you do only during certain seasons of life. A practice is forever.

Practices are for daily use, and the more often you engage in them, the greater the benefit you receive.

The more you engage in practice consistently over time, the more the illusions of the ego dissolve, and the more your heart opens and expands.

What is more important than doing a large amount of practice in a short period of time is being consistent with your practice over time.

The results of practice are cumulative. The more consistent you are, the more gifts you are bestowed.

Practice offers many gifts, including greater presence, centeredness, and acceptance; increased peace, freedom, and compassion; and deeper levels of connection, forgiveness, and love.

Practice can help to dissolve rigidity and increase flexibility.

Practice allows you to move through daily life more deeply grounded in your true nature and more deeply connected to the center of your being.

The human mind forgets over and over again, so you must help it to remember over and over again.

Reading about truth, love, and the Divine can be deeply supportive on the path, but practice is needed to truly experience them.

The purpose of practice is to support you in being present in the moment with yourself and the Divine, to allow yourself to be present with any feelings, truths, or realizations that want your attention, and to support you in remembering and returning home to Love.

Certain practices can even miraculously lessen the effects of past karma, though it is the grace of the Beloved that ultimately makes this so.

There is not one practice that is better than another. All practices and paths lead to the same place—it is simply a matter of which practices resonate most for you.

All practice leads you home.

Your practice need not be something you are rigid about. Practice is not meant to be a prison. Discipline is important so that you can engage in practice consistently, but discipline is different than being domineering. Discipline is meant to serve you, not trap you.

The amount of discipline practice requires is small compared to the freedom and love it bestows upon you.

Be gentle with yourself when you do not show up for your practice or when you are distracted the whole way through. These moments are natural and offer an opportunity for greater acceptance, self-compassion, and understanding.

Being gentle and loving with yourself supports your ability to stay consistent over time, one day at a time. Even a few minutes each day is a tangible way to care for yourself, your relationships, and your life.

Eventually, not doing practice will feel more difficult than creating the space for it.

Eventually, not doing practice will feel more uncomfortable than the ego's discomfort during it.

Eventually, all of daily life becomes a practice.

Eventually, every moment of your life becomes a prayer.

The more you do practice, the more every moment reveals itself to be an opportunity to awaken to your true being.

The purpose of practice is to see the truth.

The purpose of practice is to open your heart.

The purpose of practice is to remember and return home to Love.

If you do not currently have any practices you enjoy, explore and see what resonates for you.

It does not matter where you practice, what practices you choose, or how long you practice for. What matters is that you consistently make space in your daily life to be present with yourself, truth, and Love.

Practice improves the relationship you have with yourself, others, and the Divine.

Practice serves as a bridge that carries you to surrender.

Your practice will steadily support you throughout your entire life. It will offer you boundless love, grounding, guidance, awareness, and care.

Practice is the gift that keeps on giving.

The gifts of practice are endless, and they continue to deepen over time.

PRACTICE ACCEPTING
THE PRESENT MOMENT
INSTEAD OF RESISTING IT

"Neither seek nor avoid, take what comes."
—Swami Vivekananda

YOUR PRESENT MOMENT always exists to support your deepest healing and most expanded evolution.

What life asks you to navigate in each moment is never random.

What arises in your reality does so with great purpose and meaning.

Evolution and expansion are only available to you in the present moment.

Thoughts of past or future can cloud your mind, attempting to steal the now moment away from you—but it is only the present moment where healing and liberation can occur.

The ego seeks comfort, avoidance, and control, often resisting the present moment.

The soul desires presence, truth, and love.

When you are present in the moment, you allow yourself to connect with your body and your breath.

When you are present in the moment, you allow yourself to connect with your feelings, needs, and the desires of your soul.

When you are present in the moment, you allow yourself to navigate the challenges of daily life with greater awareness, acceptance, and surrender.

Being present in the moment supports you in being aware of the opportunity for evolution that your reality is offering to you.

The present moment is rich with potential.

The present moment is ripe with opportunity.

It is in the present moment that you can respond in a new way, communicate more respectfully, or choose to support yourself with greater care.

You do not have to be the same person you were just a moment ago. It is in the present moment that you can choose to perceive differently, behave differently, and evolve in real time.

Accepting your present moment creates space for patience to arise.

It allows you to become the witness, observing your reality instead of being taken over by it.

As you become the witness, you remember that you are not your life, you are not your personality, and you are not the experiences you encounter.

You are the consciousness that witnesses it all.

You are awareness.

You are loving awareness.

While the future may seem to promise greater peace, freedom, or joy, you are only able to access such qualities by connecting with them now. Nothing outside of you can ultimately fulfill you, as peace, freedom, and joy lie within.

Your mind may tell you that daily life is mundane, but it is the very experiences of daily life that you incarnated for.

The happenings of your daily life are divinely designed, providing the exact experiences you need to evolve in the precise ways your soul desires.

It is through the experiences of daily life that you evolve.

Every present moment in your life is designed to support your unique healing and return home to Love.

It is only in the present moment that you can be aware of the love that you are and the Love that guides you.

When you are present in the moment, you cooperate with the evolution your soul desires and take the most direct route towards your destiny.

PRACTICE ALLOWING
OTHERS TO BE AS THEY ARE

"By enduring the difficulties that arise when people from different places, of different upbringing, and temperament are thrown together, one's power of forbearance grows strong, the capacity for endurance is developed." —Anandamayi Ma

EVERY PERSON ALIGNS with and is guided by different beliefs.

The beliefs we resonate with depend on our personal karma, past history, present circumstances, and where we are in our soul's evolution.

Allow your intuition to lead you to the beliefs that feel most aligned for you.

When our personal beliefs differ from those we interact and connect with, we need not try to forcefully impose our beliefs onto them.

Your beliefs can guide you, but allow ultimate truth to be your guiding light.

Ultimate truth is love.

In connecting with others, we give them our presence and loving attention.

We encourage them to explore their own inner wisdom and align with the truths and philosophies that support their healing and evolution.

Sometimes what works for one person is the exact opposite of what works for another.

Each person chooses what feels most aligned for them at any moment in time.

If someone's beliefs awaken deep pain within you, practice discernment, not judgement.

Feel the pain.

Pray on it.

Let the Divine lead.

When we show up as a presence of love, we hold space for the other person to remember the love that they truly are.

Align with the beliefs that are grounded in your values and move through life radiating your unique essence.

Allow yourself to be guided by the wisdom that fills your heart with love.

Allow yourself to be guided by that which makes life sacred.

When connecting with others, practice doing so with respect, love, and care.

Practice accepting every being as they are, knowing that their soul is on a journey and their life is a movement of its own.

Practice accepting others with the knowing that we are all one.

May you live in alignment with truth.

May you be guided by love.

May you remember that the source of all things is forever and always guiding each of us home.

SPACE, STILLNESS, AND SILENCE ARE MEDICINES THAT HELP YOU RETURN HOME TO TRUTH AND LOVE

"Look, what is there in this world? Absolutely nothing that is lasting; therefore direct your longing towards the Eternal."
—*Anandamayi Ma*

IN TODAY'S FAST-PACED WORLD, being endlessly busy is seen as normal and is often even celebrated.

But this is the way of the ego, and not the way of the heart.

In busyness, you are led to distract and disconnect from self, others, and Spirit.

Being busy allows you to avoid your feelings, intuitions, yearnings, and truth.

In contrast, space, stillness, and silence support you in being present with your heart, spirit, and soul.

They support you in offering acknowledgement, attention, and love to the parts of you that need it.

They create room to be with what longs to arise from the center of your being.

Space, stillness, and silence are ancient medicines that help you return home to Love and the truth of who you are.

Space is both physical and energetic. Whether it is space alone with yourself or space in your day to tend to yourself, space provides you with a necessary moment in time to connect with your inner world and the center of your being.

Space supports you in returning to yourself and God.

It allows you to care for and nurture your needs on all levels.

Creating space for yourself may look like sitting outside and breathing, doing a daily practice, or taking time in the evening to unwind and come home to yourself.

Creating space for yourself is a sacred act of dedication, self-love, and self-care.

In stillness, you are able to breathe, feel, and pray in any way you desire.

You are free to give yourself exactly what you need in the moment to release, purify, and remember.

Stillness need not mean the absence of any movement at all, but rather being in such a way that promotes the presence of stillness within.

Silence supports you in moving beyond illusion and returning to all that is true.

Ramakrishna taught that "silence is the language of God."

When silence brings discomfort, something within desires your attention.

Meeting discomfort creates space for comfort to arise.

Allowing what is within you to arise in presence and with

acceptance supports you in releasing, letting go, and surrendering.

It allows you to discharge the burden of all that you carry.

Let it come to the surface, and then let it go.

Over and over again.

What has been taken in and experienced must rise to the surface to be released.

Eventually, you will be carried to a silence that nourishes and expands you.

Silence for you might include a meditation or gentle music. What matters is that your space supports you in being present with yourself and the treasure that lies within.

What matters most is that you become present enough to hear the voice of your heart, truth, and Love.

Space allows you to tune into your inner world.

Stillness allows you to meet yourself in compassion, honesty, and love.

Silence allows you to awaken to your truest being.

The more you cultivate care for your inner world, the more you become a vessel for peace and compassion.

Space, stillness, and silence support you in becoming aware of what your soul truly needs and desires.

They support you in moving from ego to soul.

Space, stillness, and silence guide you home to the truth of who you are.

They guide you home to Eternal Love and the fabric of all of existence.

ACKNOWLEDGMENT IS A PRACTICE OF DEVOTION

"Be like the honeybee who gathers only nectar wherever it goes. Seek the goodness that is found in everyone." —Amma

WHEN YOU ACKNOWLEDGE THE BEAUTY, love, and grace in your life, your acknowledgment becomes a practice of devotion.

Devotion opens your heart.

Devotion leads you from ego to soul.

Devotion returns you to all that is real.

It guides you back to your true nature.

When you honor what you receive, through others or through the Divine, your acknowledgement serves as a form of gratitude and respect.

It serves as reverence for the blessings of your life.

When you consciously take time to be present with that which you are given and that which you receive, you allow your heart to open and your gratitude to grow.

When you create space to recognize the grace in your daily life, you are carried home to Love.

Acknowledgement is not only a powerful act of respect, but it allows you to honor the beauty and support that arises in your world.

When you acknowledge the kindness, compassion, or support of another, you honor the grace of the Divine at play in its many forms.

Something as seemingly simple as eating breakfast is, in fact, not simple at all. One can acknowledge and thank the plants, animals, and people who made the meal possible; the land, air, rain, and sunshine that grew the plants; the farmworkers, truck drivers, and store employees that all played a crucial part in the meal; those who created the utensils and dish being used; the money to purchase the groceries, the space to eat in, and the body that knows how to eat and digest the food.

The amount of grace that goes into a single meal is profound, and taking a moment to acknowledge all that contributes to it is a practice that deepens your awareness of Love.

Even the smallest acts of acknowledgment become gateways to devotion, connecting the seemingly ordinary to the Divine.

Even the smallest acts of acknowledgment become gateways to devotion, connecting the seemingly ordinary to the Divine.

Saying thank you for the guidance, care, and wisdom you receive honors and connects you to the formless Love from which they arise.

Appreciation and gratitude help to dissolve the ego, return you to truth, and carry you home to Love.

The miracle of acknowledgement is that the more you practice it, the deeper your appreciation grows: for yourself, others, and your life.

The more you practice saying thank you, the more aware you become of reasons to be thankful.

During challenging times, it is natural for gratitude to feel much more difficult to practice, yet these are the very instances it can support you the most—not to bypass the pain, but to support you in it.

You can look for things to be grateful for, no matter how seemingly small.

A soft blanket, a cup of hot tea, or the sound of the breeze moving through the trees.

By turning your focus to that which you are grateful for, you can connect with Love in the midst of your pain.

Practice noticing compassion, beauty, or kindness in yourself, others, and the world around you.

Through acknowledgement, you transform your daily life into a practice of devotion.

You see that life is a gift you have been given.

You see that every breath is a gift from God.

When you seek truth, you find truth.

When you seek Love, you see Love.

Acknowledgement opens your heart.

Acknowledgment deepens your awareness of oneness.

Acknowledgment returns you to the knowing that this is a loving universe and you are infinitely held, guided, and supported.

PRAYER IS A DOORWAY TO THE DIVINE

"Prayer is the medium of miracles."
—*A Course in Miracles*

LIFE WAS NOT DESIGNED for you to navigate alone.

You are not alone and you could never be alone.

Divine Love desires to care for you, support you, and guide you.

Like a perfect and unconditionally loving parent, the Divine desires to help you in miraculous ways, always and forever for your highest good.

But you must first ask for the help you desire.

In the same way that communication can deeply nourish a relationship, making conscious effort to communicate and connect with the Divine profoundly nurtures your connection with it.

Prayer is not about asking for the things your ego desires, but about making conscious contact with Divine Love—consciously connecting with your deepest being, the light of awareness, and the all-abiding presence of love.

Prayer guides you to the knowing that you are always given exactly what is needed in every single moment.

It is an action that, when earnestly taken, supports you in going beyond the ego, personality, and mind, and into the heart, into truth, and into Love.

Spiritual wisdom teaches not to pray for the dissolution of challenges, but rather for the strength, wisdom, and courage needed to navigate the situations you find yourself in.

Such is the prayer of the soul—understanding that through hardship one can purify, open the heart, and realize God.

Prayer is a pathway back to the love that you are.

It supports you in asking for help and remembering that you are not alone.

It assists you in connecting with yourself and others.

Prayer supports you in releasing judgment and resentment.

It helps you to open your heart and dissolve the walls of the ego.

Prayer supports you in surrendering and centering.

It assists you in receiving help and embracing divine guidance.

It supports you in serving and in setting intentions.

Prayer supports you in offering gratitude.

It supports you in being present and grounding into trust.

Prayer supports you in returning home to Love.

There is no one right way to pray.

Pray in the ways that feel aligned for you.

You can speak internally or aloud.

You can get on your knees to pray (a powerful position of humility and surrender, both of which deepen the sincerity of your prayer) or pray while moving about (a beautiful way to remain connected to God throughout the day).

You can write your prayers down or speak them over a fire.

You can sing your prayers or paint them upon a canvas.

You can make an offering to whomever you are praying to—such as flowers, a song, fruit, chocolate, or simply a glass of water. It matters not what you offer, but the sincerity and purity of heart with which you offer it.

You can create a ritual or ceremony to pray. It need not be elaborate, unless you wish it to be. The lighting of a candle, a heartfelt prayer, and an offering is enough.

You can create an altar with something to represent each element, along with a photo of a deity, enlightened being, or saint.

You can even pray by weeping. When asked what is the easiest way to God, Ananadamayi Ma responded, "Profuse tears."

There is no one right way to pray, as long as your prayers are sincere. God cannot ignore a prayer from a pure and open heart.

The Divine does not care how you pray, only that your heart be loving and your prayers be pure.

Pray in the ways that resonate for you.

You can pray anytime, anywhere.

You can pray in any way and for however long you desire.

When you pray, get behind your prayer—meaning, once you

offer your prayer, trust it will be answered in divine timing and in the ways that are most aligned for your highest good.

Prayer allows you to awaken to, open to, and receive miracles.

It grounds you into love, guides you with love, and empowers you to lead with love.

Through prayer, you receive love and recognize Love.

Prayer is a superpower granted to you by the Beloved to connect with the Beloved.

Prayer leads you back to the love that you are, the Divine Love within you.

Prayer is simple.

Prayer is profound.

Prayer helps you return home to all that is true.

The more you pray, the more you awaken to the Love within and all around you.

OFFER YOUR ACTIONS TO GOD

"All action is prayer."
—*Neem Karoli Baba*

THROUGH THE OFFERING of your actions to God, your daily life becomes a spiritual practice.

When you offer your actions to the Divine, you align your will with divine will and release attachment to the outcomes.

You see yourself as a vessel and allow God to move through you.

Offering your actions involves dedicating your actions to the Divine, one moment at a time, in order to allow Love to move you, while releasing attachment to any specific result.

Through the offering of your actions to the Divine, even the simplest of actions, like brushing your teeth or making your bed, can become a sacred opportunity for devotion.

Action grounded in duty, dharma, and love is an offering to God.

Aligning your actions with divine will allows you to live with greater dignity, trust, and peace.

Aligning your actions with a higher order always benefits the whole.

When you view your actions as pathways to God, each one becomes a prayer.

No effort expended is ever wasted, despite the outcome. Your mind may disagree, but it does not know the truth.

When you offer your actions to God, you live in alignment with Love's will for you, one moment at a time.

When you offer your actions to God, you act from a place of selflessness, responsibility, and devotion. You perform your actions as best you can, without attachment to the outcome.

When you offer your actions, both big and small, your daily life becomes a prayer.

There is no action too small or feeling too painful that cannot be offered.

It is not only actions that can be offered, but feelings and experiences, as well.

Practice continuously offering everything to the Divine—your grief, gratitude, rage, and doubt.

Your suffering, your healing, your laughter, and your fear.

When you offer it all to God, you use everything as a way to get free.

You transform everything into an act of devotion.

To offer your actions to the Divine is to understand that you are an instrument of Divine Love, acting for Divine Love, and the results are not yours to carry.

When your actions are done from a place of love and

responsibility, free from ego and attachment to the results, they purify you.

The *Bhagavad Gita* teaches that through offering and dedicating your actions to the One, you become freed from the karma they create.

Even pleasurable karma is still karma that can keep you bound in the cycle of life and death, but when you offer your actions to the Divine, you begin to be released from this endless cycle.

When you notice your actions are not grounded in dharma or love, you can still offer them up, as well. In fact, this is an especially aligned time to do so, as this offering returns you home to Love.

When you notice you have strayed from love, whether in thought or action, simply choose to return to love once again.

You will see that it was never Love that left, but only you who turned away.

Choosing love means choosing compassion.

Choosing love means choosing patience.

Choosing love means choosing to see the One in all.

When you allow yourself to be guided by true wisdom, you are no longer led by the desires of the ego, but by the desire of the soul to return to the source of all that is.

When you navigate life in alignment with divine will, you are carried to levels of acceptance, surrender, and peace your mind did not even know existed.

See your actions not as chores or checklists, but as sacred invitations to remember the Divine.

Daily actions then become sacred opportunities to make offerings and remember God.

Do your duties, both large and small, with devotion and offer your entire being to the Beloved.

Your daily life can be a constant invitation back to spirit.

Your daily life can be a constant invitation back home to Love.

Return to the present moment.

Return to the seat of your heart.

Allow your daily life to become the sacred vessel for the evolution of your soul.

When you offer everything that you are, everything that you do, and everything that you have to the Beloved, you live in constant devotion.

Your life becomes a way to remember.

Your daily life becomes a prayer.

LIVE YOUR DHARMA

"It is better to live your own Dharma imperfectly than to live another's Dharma perfectly." —Bhagavad Gita

IN THE ANCIENT and sacred Hindu text, the *Bhagavad Gita*, a number of virtues are taught as essential to honor and live by, in order to attain true peace and liberation.

One of its main teachings is on dharma, or one's duty in life.

Dharma is guided by the Divine and encompasses living in alignment with your true nature, responsibilities, and purpose. Dharma takes into account your various roles, relationships, and abilities.

Dharma can include karma yoga, which is the path of selfless action. Karma yoga involves doing one's duties and serving others without any attachment to the results. It teaches that one should fulfill one's dharma because it is the Divine's will, and release attachment to the fruits of one's actions.

When you live your dharma and act in harmony with cosmic order, you align yourself and your actions with truth and love.

When you live your dharma, you live in alignment with the Divine's will for you.

When you live your dharma, you take the actions you took this birth to perform.

In our modern world, the concept of dharma is rarely taught and not often spoken about.

To live without this teaching would be a monumental disservice to your soul's journey.

There are a variety of different kinds of dharma, including your personal dharma and your universal dharma.

Your personal dharma comprises honoring the roles and responsibilities you have been assigned in this lifetime.

Your personal dharma involves honoring your natural abilities, gifts, nature, and duties in order to live in alignment with God's will for you in this incarnation.

Personal dharma includes caring for yourself and others, living in alignment with moral and ethical responsibilities, and fulfilling familial and professional responsibilities.

When you live your dharma, you live in alignment with your soul's purpose in this birth.

When you live your dharma, you honor divine order.

When you live your dharma, you surrender to what Love wants for you.

Love always knows best.

Your ego may resist your dharma, but it is your path to freedom.

It is natural for the ego to resist dharma out of fear. Yet, when you live in accordance with Love's will for you, you support the entire universe in returning home to Love.

The gifts and responsibilities you have been bestowed in this lifetime come with great purpose.

Your gifts are designed to support yourself and the collective.

The fulfillment of your duties serves the whole.

Dharma can look like caring for a child, pet, or elder.

Dharma can look like sharing your art.

Dharma can look like living the life that is meant for you, no matter how scary it may feel.

When you understand what your dharma is, you stop swimming upstream and begin moving in alignment with divine flow.

You begin to feel supported by the entire universe.

You begin to see where Supreme Wisdom intends for you to be.

Understanding your dharma makes living in alignment with divine will infinitely easier.

Understanding your dharma allows you to surrender to Love's will for you, one moment at a time.

It allows you to accept your personal and professional responsibilities with greater ease and grace.

It allows you to make decisions with deeper clarity and direction.

When you take the actions God intends for you, you can release attachment to their results, knowing that you did exactly as you were designed to.

When you know your actions are guided by the Divine, you need not worry about the outcome.

A balanced mind understands that both failure and success are natural aspects of the human experience.

The *Bhagavad Gita* teaches the importance of performing your duties without fear of failure, as fear itself is a source of suffering. It helps us see that a life well lived is a life rooted in dharma, regardless of the outcome.

Surrender any fears and have faith that you are exactly where Love wants you to be.

Focus on the effort you put into your actions, and not the final results.

When you perform your actions with selflessness and care, without attachment to the outcome, you purify and attain true wisdom.

When you offer your actions to the Divine, your connection with Divine Love deepens.

Universal dharma includes living with honesty, integrity, compassion, and equanimity.

Universal dharma involves navigating life with humility, respect, and continuous spiritual learning, in order to support the evolution of your soul.

Universal dharma involves honoring the connection between all beings, the purpose of all things, and the recognition of your true Self.

In the *Bhagavad Gita*, recognizing your true nature is taught to be the ultimate purpose of every being.

To awaken to the Divine within.

To see that you are not your body, feelings, or thoughts.

To see that you are not what happened to you, the pain you carry, or the limitations you experience, but to know that you are flowing and formless love.

A miraculous creation of the Divine.

Eternal and unchanging.

True dharma does not benefit oneself only; it always benefits the whole.

When you align with your dharma, you live in alignment with truth.

When you live your dharma, you return yourself and all of existence home to Love.

TAKE RESPONSIBILITY
IN YOUR LIFE

"A saint is a sinner who never gave up."
—*Paramahansa Yogananda*

SELF-RESPONSIBILITY IS an essential aspect of living a healthy and fulfilling life.

Acknowledging your part in the situations you face and tending to your side of the street supports you in deepening in humility, self-trust, and self-love.

It supports you in embodying the inherent power of the Divine within.

As you move through life, do you often blame others for the pain and problems you experience, or do you regularly take responsibility for your part in what arises?

Do you acknowledge and clean up your part in things?

You entered this incarnation with particular karmas, circumstances, and experiences to navigate in order to evolve in the ways your soul desires.

Your life is asking you to take responsibility.

The phrase "take responsibility" may stir resistance within you, and that is okay. Acknowledge it, allow it to be there, and then notice what lies beneath it.

When you acknowledge the power you have in the situations you experience, both internally and externally, you are able to move through challenges with greater power and grace.

Responsibility is a sign of maturity.

Taking responsibility moves your life in the direction of your desires far more quickly than blame, shame, or helplessness does. In fact, those patterns only hold you back.

That being said, sometimes we need to fall into these patterns of the ego that are rooted in fear and separation, in order to remember the way to get back home.

The relationship you have with yourself and others drastically improves the more responsibility you take for what arises.

Blame shuts down vulnerability and places the focus on the other, instead of on the aspects of self and life that are yours to tend to.

Complaining is a substitute for asking.

Where might you be complaining instead of asking for what you need?

Where might you be complaining instead of acknowledging your part in the issue?

Reflect on the ways your mind attempts to avoid taking responsibility.

Are you blaming others instead of acknowledging your part?

Are you giving your power away instead of acting from the God-given strength within you?

Do you need to communicate a boundary, feel your feelings, engage in practice, or ask for help?

Shift your focus from the other's faults and reflect on what you can do to improve the situation for yourself.

You are not to blame for the circumstances you face, but you are responsible for the healing you require—and remember, you need never be alone in this process.

Taking responsibility may mean determining what is yours and what is not yours to carry.

It may mean supporting yourself in the ways you need so as not to hold the pain others place upon you.

It may mean embracing yourself in care, self-love, and compassion.

When you notice you are blaming, shaming, or pointing the finger towards others, turn the focus back to yourself.

When you recognize you are giving your power away, practice embodying the strength of the Divine that lives within you.

Reflect on how you can take greater responsibility for your inner world, including your thoughts, perceptions, feelings, and beliefs.

Reflect on how you can take greater responsibility for your outer world, including your self-care, communication, actions, and relationships.

Are you telling yourself stories of victimization, helplessness, and shame?

Or are you choosing to bathe yourself in compassion, empowerment, and love?

As interdependent beings, we are designed to lean on one another and receive support, but interdependence also involves self-responsibility.

It asks us to take care of our side of the street and what is within our control.

Self-responsibility includes how we speak to and about ourselves, how we care for ourselves, how we relate to others, and how we shape the stories we tell.

When we make a mistake or find ourselves in conflict, self-responsibility asks us to reflect, respond, and repair, rather than deny, blame, or shame.

It invites us to look at our part in a situation. Perhaps it is what we did or did not say, our tone, expectations, lack of honesty, or the way we placed our pain onto another.

In situations of great pain, trauma, or injustice, responsibility may simply look like the courageous act of asking for the help you are worthy of.

Taking responsibility demonstrates a well of strength, humility, and self-awareness. It does not ever mean to blame yourself, but rather to ask, "Is there something I can learn here? What was my part? What can I do differently next time?"

There is always a reason that a specific situation arises in your life. When you reflect on your part or how it can help you grow, you are able to move through the experience in a more empowered and productive way.

Every situation carries an opportunity for healing. Taking responsibility for your growth allows you to receive the gifts each circumstance offers.

Self-responsibility brings greater self-trust and self-esteem into your life.

It allows you to experience greater peace, freedom, and joy.

When you relinquish responsibility, life often speaks louder and louder until you are willing to listen.

When you begin to take responsibility for what you do have control over, your life powerfully transforms.

Remember, you are not meant to do any of this alone.

Pray, ask for help.

You are a child of God, and with Divine Love leading the way, you can do and navigate absolutely anything you are called to.

You can create a life of deep peace, love, and alignment.

But you must take responsibility for yourself and your life in the ways that only you can.

Go slowly. Be gentle with yourself and begin taking responsibility for your inner and outer worlds.

Begin by seeing everything as part of the dream designed to help you awaken.

Begin by recognizing the power that lives within you.

As you do so, watch your world evolve.

This is not the easy path, but it does become easier over time.

This is not the ego path, but it invites you to live your life in service of its true purpose.

Taking responsibility is a deeply humbling experience.

Humility is purifying.

Let yourself be purified.

Taking responsibility leads you to an inner well of strength and integrity.

When you take responsibility for the stories and perceptions you live by, you begin to awaken to the power within you to experience greater peace.

When you take responsibility for how you communicate, you see how much power you truly have.

When you take responsibility for your own peace and joy, you stop waiting for others to give you what only you can give to yourself.

What you desire exists within you already.

Peace is available for you now.

Love is available for you now.

HONOR THE TRUTH OF YOUR SOUL

"It isn't true that everyone should follow one path. Listen to your own truth." —*Ram Dass*

WHEN YOU ALLOW others to direct your life, you end up living in accordance with their beliefs, and not your own.

When you make decisions based on the desires of the ego, whether yours or others, you hand your precious and holy life over to illusion, rather than truth.

Living life according to the ego's wishes or making decisions based on what others want for you leaves you feeling powerless and off-path. Your life force diminished, your light dimmed.

When the desires of your soul remain hidden, the entire universe misses out on the opportunity to experience your magnificent and miraculous nature.

When you do not honor the desires of your soul, Spirit loses the great privilege to freely express itself as you.

No one can be you but you.

You took this birth to live in accordance with the desires of your soul, not another's.

God created you to experience itself as you, not someone else.

Every soul that comes to Earth has its own distinct curriculum, including specific lessons to learn and healing to undergo in each lifetime.

Every person, on their own remarkable hero's journey, is here to learn exactly what is most essential in their current phase of evolution.

What you have come here to learn in this incarnation may be completely different, or even opposite, from what another soul is here to learn.

Even when two souls come here to learn similar lessons, the ways in which those lessons unfold are entirely unique to each of them.

You know what is most aligned for you.

True knowing, however, does not at all occur in the surface-level thoughts of the mind, but rather in the depths of your heart and the sacred whispers of your soul.

True knowing is rooted in the Divine, in wisdom, and in love.

True knowing guides you to the spaces and places where you truly belong.

When you live by the truth of the ego, you descend further into separation, emptiness, and despair.

When you live by the truth of your soul, you are carried on a path of healing, miracles, and love.

Being supported on your path is a natural and healthy part of being human, as it allows you to be held, recognize blind spots, and see through the tricks of the ego. Nonetheless, even when receiving support from someone you trust, it is necessary to use your discernment and honor what ultimately feels true for you.

Your soul knows what is best for you.

Your soul knows the way back home.

The answers lie within, though they ask you to turn inward and be still in order to be heard.

Sometimes honoring your truth means disappointing others.

Sometimes honoring your desires draws criticism.

Sometimes honoring your needs disturbs the peace.

Though when you honor what is most aligned for you, you invariably honor what is best for all souls involved, even when their egos cannot yet understand it.

Speaking up, making decisions, and living life in accordance with the truth of your heart and soul supports everyone in your life as they progress along their own soul journey.

We each learn in our own way.

We perceive differently.

We make choices using different methods.

We each serve a unique function here on Earth.

The way a particular soul walks through life may not align with your specific design in this incarnation.

You may be learning different lessons or here to serve a different role.

None is better than another, merely different.

All vastly important.

When you live in alignment with the truth of your soul, you serve the highest good of all beings.

When you live in alignment with the desires of your soul, you help return not only yourself, but all of existence, home to Love.

YOUR TRUTH IS SACRED

"One must be very particular about telling the truth. Through truth one can realize God." —Ramakrishna

YOUR TRUTH IS SACRED.

The desires of your soul are holy.

Your yes's and no's exist to lead you to the spaces and places where you truly belong.

They are internal messages from the Divine, lovingly guiding you along your path.

Allow your likes, dislikes, passions, and interests to lead you.

Your inner knowings exist with great purpose and reason.

They exist to guide you home.

It is essential, however, to continuously tune in and discern whether a yes or no is arising from your ego or your soul.

Amma teaches to be aware of the deceptions of the mind. She

says, "The mind will keep playing its tricks. It has so many ways to do so."

The ego can be quite cunning and attempt to steer you away from that which is most aligned for you. Filled with separating desires, it can lure you towards distraction and away from the desires of your soul.

The ego, feeling separate from Love, speaks loudly, fearfully, and urgently. At times it may sound certain and commanding, and other times steeped in confusion and distress.

Your soul, your true knowing, speaks quietly, calmly, and lovingly.

Your soul communicates with complete trust because it is the part of you that has never forgotten it is pure Divine Love.

Your soul speaks peacefully, as it is not in a rush and has nothing to prove.

That being said, continuously ignoring your truth or intuition can cause louder and louder calls for you to honor it, such as physical, emotional, mental, or spiritual symptoms.

Your yes's and no's can be felt in your body.

A no can feel like contraction, constriction, or closing off. It can feel like tension, aversion, or pushing away.

A no can bring feelings of uneasiness, a sense that something feels off, or the inability to settle into a full-body yes.

A yes can feel like opening, releasing, and relaxing, safety, magnetism, or peace.

A yes can bring feelings of trust and ease.

Your body may offer you other unique signs into your own personal yes's and no's, such as hearing a certain sound, noticing a certain smell, or getting goosebumps.

As you make decisions, tune into the subtle signs your body may offer you, as these can greatly assist you in your decision-making process.

Beyond how a yes or no feels in your body, you may also have an intuitive knowing or sense of what is most aligned.

Remember though, the mind will play its tricks.

When confusion arises regarding which choice to make, allow the confusion to be there. Let it be okay that you do not know the answer, as that is the experience you are meant to be having at that moment in time.

The more you resist your current experience, the more uncomfortable it will be.

Simply bringing your awareness to the situation and noting that you are resisting will immediately shift the energy surrounding it.

You do not have to change anything, you do not have to do anything differently. Release the pressure of the thinking mind and simply be the witness to the experiences of your ego.

Just notice and name the experiences you are having in the present moment, allowing yourself to be and do exactly as you are. This will help to release stuck energy and free up space to be in your heart.

You can also pray. Ask for help.

You are not meant to navigate this experience alone.

Allow what is to be as it is.

The answers and next steps will arrive in divine timing and not a moment sooner.

The answers will arrive through the winds of grace.

When you make decisions out of alignment with your inner knowing, you find yourself in spaces and situations that do not feel aligned.

When you find yourself living out of alignment or feeling off-path, fear not. You are only there because there is something there for you to learn.

Making decisions out of alignment with the truth of your soul can teach you many important lessons and provide you with invaluable information.

These experiences allow you to see how your body feels when you go against your truth.

They help you become aware of how your mind responds when you go against your inner knowing.

They allow you to experience the discomfort that arises when you go against what is true for you.

All of these insights support you in honoring the truth that flows through you more fully next time a similar situation arises.

Mistakes are part of being human, and their purpose is to help us learn, heal, and evolve.

When you acknowledge and allow your yes's and no's to guide you, you take the most direct route towards your destiny.

You allow yourself to be guided by the discernment given to you by the Divine.

When you honor your inner yes and inner no, you allow yourself to be guided by Love.

You allow yourself to be guided exactly where you are meant to be.

Others may not understand. They may question, criticize, or

judge. This can feel unsettling and ungrounding, but it becomes easier to hold with trust and surrender.

Allow your faith to ground you into truth and Love.

You need not fear saying no to that which is not aligned for you.

However difficult it may feel, every no leads you to something of greater alignment.

By saying no, you create space for what is truly meant for you to enter your life.

When you are able to say a clear no, your yes's carry ever more truth, integrity, and purpose.

Your yes's and no's are here to help lead you.

They are guideposts.

They are messages from your soul and from the Divine, leading you towards your destiny.

They need not always make sense to the logical thinking mind.

When you are uncertain, pray, ask for support, and be patient.

Trust your yes's and no's.

They are sacred.

They allow you to be guided by spirit and by soul.

They allow Love to lead you home.

YOU ARE NOT THE DOER

"God alone is the doer and you are the instrument."
—*Ramakrishna*

YOU ARE NOT THE DOER.

You are an instrument of God, a vessel for the Beloved, a channel for the Divine.

Perform your duties, engage in your roles, and tend to your responsibilities, knowing all the while that it is Love that moves you.

Align your will with divine will.

Allow the Divine to move through you.

Take the necessary actions each day and in each moment, knowing all the while that the ego, the personality, and the I, is not the doer.

Divine Love is what moves you.

The ego is not in control.

The ego is not responsible for the fruits of its actions.

When you align your will with divine will, you are not responsible for the failures of your actions either.

The person you believe yourself to be is transitory.

Your true nature was created by Love and is Love, the same miraculous force within all beings and woven within all of existence.

Your consciousness is Divine Love.

You act and exist because Love wills it to be so.

When you perform your actions, it is not you who creates success or failure, judgment or praise.

When you align your will with divine will, God acts through you.

When creative inspiration moves through you, you are the conduit.

When you receive praise, success, or criticism, remember, you are not the doer.

You are the being through which Love moves, but you are not the creator of that Love.

What is sent through you and out into the world is done so by God and God alone.

You are the sacred vessel.

You cannot control the incarnation you came here to experience, but you can choose whether or not you use your life as a vehicle for evolution.

Allow the Divine to lead you, and your life will become a reflection of devotion, humility, and integrity.

Allow yourself to be guided by the One, and you will be a channel for Love in this world.

Humility, purification, and devotion are essential components of being a vessel for Love.

Be humble and know that you are not the doer.

Purify so you may be guided by truth, not ego.

Have reverence for that which moves you.

Offer gratitude for the opportunity to serve.

You are being carried with love, by Love, and for Love.

If your ego could fathom just one fragment of the perfection at play, it would instantly bow to the Love within and at the center of it all.

If your ego understood the sublime nature behind everything at play, it would cease to be afraid.

Align your will with divine will and witness the miracles that occur within and all around you.

SURRENDER IS THE WAY HOME

"You will have to go beyond the level where there is certainty and uncertainty." —*Anandamayi Ma*

WHEN YOU SURRENDER, you offer yourself and your life to the Beloved.

When you surrender, you allow the current of Love to carry you.

When you surrender, you trust Love to lead you home.

Surrender is a sheer act of courage.

It is the fastest path to where you desire to be.

Fast, however, does not necessarily mean easy.

Sometimes the pathway to surrender is fraught with resistance, and that, too, exists to help guide you home to inner peace.

Resistance can look like pushing against what is.

It can take the form of anger, fear, denial, or control.

Such experiences need not be rushed, as your process will unfold in its own time.

The *Bhagavad Gita* teaches that no effort is ever wasted, which means that any effort you make towards your evolution is forever beneficial.

Simply witnessing, bringing awareness to, and noting when you are resisting or feeling stuck is immensely valuable on your soul's journey.

Being hard on yourself for being where you are only strengthens the resistance. But witnessing it, allowing it, and accepting it frees the stuck energy, carrying you back to the river of truth, grace, and love.

Surrender occurs when you release control, stop trying to figure things out, and let go of fighting what you are moving through.

Surrender is sacred.

Surrender occurs when you finally accept your experience and the pain that it brings.

Sometimes, surrender creates space for the very pain the ego was attempting to avoid through resistance.

And still, even then, surrender is the most supportive and direct route home.

Surrender means letting go of trying to force, control, or manipulate the situation.

When you surrender, you accept what is.

You allow the current circumstances of your life to guide you through the evolution they are here to assist with.

Surrender does not mean inaction, but rather aligning your will with the will of the Divine.

To accept where you are in the present moment.

To honor the lessons Love is wanting you to learn at this moment in time.

The daily unfolding of your life exists to support your deepest healing and evolution.

When you swim upstream, attempting to go against where the current is carrying you, you do not end up where you truly long to be.

You find yourself in spaces and places that feel misaligned and fraught with obstacles.

The mind does not know better than God.

The mind can be utterly narrow, while the heart can be a vast expanse.

The mind is limited.

Love is infinite.

When you attempt to force, deny, manipulate, or control, you do not end up where your soul desires to be.

You end up far from home.

You end up feeling all alone because the illusion of separation was directing you.

The more you resist, the louder the messages must grow in order to get your attention; the greater the pain and discomfort must become until you choose to acknowledge their cause.

A crisis is Divine Love's attempt to lead you, sometimes after great resistance, to the healing and evolution your soul desires.

Sometimes a crisis opens the heart more than anything else can.

Sometimes the experiences we would never consciously choose for ourselves end up initiating profound transformation in our lives, leading to deeper presence, compassion, and faith.

You need not push against the current of Love.

Go where Love is leading you, within and without.

Love always carries you exactly where you need to be, at precisely the right time.

The mind has never known better, does not know better, and will never know better than Love.

The smoothest path to the place you long to be is to surrender and allow the current of Love to carry you.

The current circumstances of your life would not exist if they were not supporting your soul evolution.

As your relationship with the Divine deepens, you begin to see that not having faith brings far more fear, chaos, and turmoil than having it does.

The formless, timeless, and boundless source of all of creation can be trusted.

It is only the ego that fears.

You are exactly where you are supposed to be.

Trust that which created you and allow it to lead you.

Trust the core of your being.

Surrender yourself to the Divine.

Offer yourself to the Beloved.

Let Love lead.

Trust where you are placed in every holy moment.

Remember, you are human and you are not here to do any of this perfectly. Rather, these are paths to help guide you home, over and over again.

Your human predicament and your divine nature are all part of your journey here.

It is all welcome.

It is all loved.

The questioning, fear, and doubt,

The hopelessness, shame, and rage.

None of it is bad or wrong.

There is space for all of you to be exactly as you are, in the complete fullness of your being.

All of it is sacred.

Offer it all to the Divine.

Allow yourself to be divinely guided.

When you notice you are resisting or that your mind is leading the way, that awareness alone can help free you from the bondage of the ego.

When you acknowledge and honor the messages and lessons appearing in your reality, you allow yourself to be guided by Love.

When you allow Love to carry you, even when it feels overwhelmingly difficult to do so, you know that whatever you are called to navigate is exactly what you must move through.

Trust and faith allow you to remember that you are divinely held, loved, and supported, and that challenges and pain are transitory and never the truth of who you are.

You can trust the current of Love.

No matter how rocky the river may seem, these waters always carry you home.

When you surrender, you allow yourself to trust-fall into the arms of the Beloved.

You allow yourself to be carried by that which always honors your highest and greatest good.

In surrender, you are like a feather being carried by the wind, a wind that knows exactly where and how to lead you in every single moment with absolute perfection.

Such divine guidance can be wholly trusted.

Surrender allows you to find yourself in spaces and places your mind could never lead you to or even imagine.

Surrender allows you to be guided not by ego, but only by Love.

Love always knows best.

Love always leads you home.

DIVINE TIMING CANNOT BE RUSHED, BUT YOU CAN TRUST IT WHOLEHEARTEDLY

"Whatever is destined not to happen will not happen, try hard how you may. Whatever is destined to happen will happen, do what you may to stop it. This is certain." —Ramana Maharshi

PRACTICE LETTING GO of the need to know how it all turns out.

Practice releasing control, one moment and one breath at a time.

There is a master plan at play here, and it is far beyond what your human mind could even begin to conceive.

The path may not unfold how your mind wishes it to, but it is the path you need to evolve in the precise ways your soul desires.

Everything in your life exists to support you, including the timing of that which you desire.

There is purpose in all, even when the ego cannot see or understand it.

When it feels difficult to surrender, turn to practices that support you in trusting and grounding into truth and Love.

Act only when it feels divinely inspired and aligned to do so, and aside from that, simply breathe, trust, and let go, over and over again.

Return to the peace that you are.

Return to the knowing that everything is exactly as it must be in this now moment.

Release your attachment to the outcome.

Trust in that which carries you and that from which you came.

Divine timing knows best.

Divine timing is the highest timeline for your lifetime.

You are exactly where you are supposed to be.

You are being divinely guided.

You are cared for, carried, and supported.

You can trust the timing of your life.

You can trust the timing of Love.

TRUST PERIODS OF
COMPLETE UNKNOWN

"If you knew who walks beside you on the way that you have chosen, fear would be impossible." —A Course in Miracles

WHEN YOU ARE PLACED in a period of complete unknown, it is always with great purpose.

When you are placed in a period of complete unknown, it is always for your highest good.

In times of immense uncertainty, you are not being asked to force, control, or manipulate the situation.

In times of complete unknown, you are being asked to surrender.

You are being asked to let go.

During times of uncertainty, you are being guided to ground deeply into trust.

You are being asked to be okay with not knowing.

You are being asked to have faith in the Divine.

Mystery, uncertainty, and the unknown are inherent in this being human. There is so much we do not know, and life is intentionally designed that way.

We must honor the great mystery, rather than try to force knowing, control outcomes, or manipulate our understanding of that which cannot be understood.

When you find yourself in a period of complete unknown, know that you are being cared for, carried, and held every single step of the way.

You are never alone, not for a single moment.

You are being asked to trust in that which loves you.

Support yourself in the ways that most deeply resonate for you.

Call upon the support of the Divine and others.

Engage in practice.

Spend time in the embrace of nature.

Continuously ground back into truth, love, and all that is real.

Allow yourself to be supported as you surrender into the mystery of your holy existence.

Allow yourself to be guided by the miracle of Love.

Love is here now.

Love is guiding you.

Love is within the period of complete unknown.

Love is what awaits you on the other side, as well.

There is profound power in being able to rest in the unknown.

When you find yourself in the depths of mystery, know that

miracles await you; but you must sail on the ship of your faith in order to receive them.

Rest in the unknown, and in time, you will see that Love was carrying you all along.

When you surrender and trust the Divine to guide you, you arrive somewhere beyond what your thinking mind could ever imagine.

Trust the great mystery.

Trust that Love is leading you home.

When you let Love lead, you are never led astray.

When you let Love lead, you always end up exactly where you are meant to be.

YOU NEED ONLY
KNOW THE NEXT STEP

"You can plan for a hundred years, but you don't know what will happen the next moment." —*Neem Karoli Baba*

THE EXPERIENCE of being human requires action. Even during periods of complete surrender and unknown, action must be taken.

The action may be simple, such as sitting in stillness, making a cup of tea, or praying.

Or, depending on your circumstances, the action may feel more complex, such as meeting distressing emotions, initiating a difficult conversation, or making a life-changing decision.

Whatever it may be, the next aligned step is all that is needed. The following step will reveal itself when it is time.

The very next step, the next aligned action to take, is revealed moment by moment.

The beautiful thing is that you never ever have to decide what the next action is on your own, as the Divine is always and forever here to lead you.

When you do not know what to do, turn your attention to the Divine and ask to be guided.

Your experience here on Earth asks you to surrender into the well of your faith.

You need only know the next step on your path.

You do not need to know the endpoint or every single step you will take to get there.

Even when you think you know, unexpected twists and turns will arise.

The ego desires a concrete plan of predictable steps and controllable outcomes, but this is not the way life unfolds.

The ego feels safe and in control in the known. Driven by fear, it tries to force, push, and manipulate to get what it wants. Yet this only leads you further from where your soul truly desires to be.

Your soul trusts, allows, and surrenders.

Your soul knows the mysteries of life are always leading you home.

Allow Love to lead the way.

If the direction should change, trust that the Divine is guiding you exactly where you are meant to be.

The next step on your path will reveal itself when it is time.

If you do not yet know what it is, then it is not yet time to know.

The answers will come in divine timing.

For now, take the next aligned action, one moment at a time.

When you allow inner wisdom to point the way, you allow yourself to be guided by Supreme Truth.

You allow yourself to be guided by the One.

One step at a time, you arrive somewhere beyond what your thinking mind could ever imagine.

Everything you need for your evolution in this moment is already here for you right now.

It is safe to trust.

It is safe to surrender.

It is safe to let Love lead you home.

FEAR IS A THRESHOLD GUARDIAN

"Courage is a very important thing."
—*Neem Karoli Baba*

FEAR THAT ARISES during times of expansion and evolution serves as a threshold guardian, testing your commitment to yourself, your duty, and your dharma.

This type of fear arises when you are at the threshold of the known world and the unknown world.

This type of fear is a sign that you are in the exact right place, at the exact right time.

The ego resists expansion because it is afraid.

The ego is often like a small child who is fearful of the unknown. You can have compassion for the child, but you do not let its fear lead.

Because the mind is grounded in fear, it does not know the way back home.

When you are expanding, evolving, and entering new spaces, both internally and externally, the mind will give you every reason to shut the movement down.

To constrict, contract, and become small.

The ego does not like expansion because it cannot control, predict, or direct it.

The ego does not like expansion because it does not feel safe in what is unfamiliar.

The ego wants nothing to do with expansion,

But the soul wants everything to do with it.

Your soul took this birth to evolve.

As you heal and grow, the ego will attempt to keep you from that which is most supportive for you.

The ego is not bad, but it often tries to lead you astray.

Your mind may feed you stories of unworthiness, inferiority, or danger to keep you from the experiences and growth to which you are being called.

It may create convincing stories of rationalization and justification to steer you off path.

It may even feed you thoughts of superiority and self-righteousness, in an extra tricky attempt to keep you from that which is most supportive and aligned for you.

Feel the fear and do it anyway, but be sure you are supported along the way.

This fear is a sign you are expanding.

This fear is a sign you are exactly where you are supposed to be.

Fear is an invitation back to your heart, back to truth, and back to love.

Engage in practice to support you in navigating the fear.

Have trusted others assist you in facing the fear.

But feel the fear and continue moving forward, one step and one moment at a time.

Easy does it, but do it.

Acting with courage does not mean acting without fear; it means feeling afraid and acting despite it.

Feeling afraid yet still taking action connects you to trust, faith, and the Divine.

Saying yes to aligned expansion helps you to release illusion and return home to Love.

It aligns your will with divine will and allows you to be held and supported by cosmic order and Universal Love.

The results of your actions are not for you to be concerned with.

Release attachment to the outcome, knowing that you are exactly where you are meant to be.

Performing your divinely assigned duties supports your spiritual evolution and progress on your path towards liberation.

When you act in alignment with God's will for you, you support both yourself and all beings in returning home to Love.

WHEN A CHALLENGE ARISES, HAND THE SITUATION OVER TO GOD

"Where God may place you at any time and under whatever circumstances, recollect that it is all for the best. Endeavor to go through life leaving your burdens in His hands."
—Anandamayi Ma

THE SOUL DOES NOT ACT with urgency.

The soul exists in perfect peace, patience, and presence.

The way of the ego is to fear, force, and control.

The way of the soul is to trust, surrender, and have faith.

Surrender is always the most direct route to where you desire to be.

When a difficult situation arises, hand it over to God.

Do not bear the burden alone.

Ask for help.

Pray, practice, and remember.

Release illusion and return to truth.

Allow yourself to be carried in the arms of the Divine, towards all that is true and all that is love.

When you hand your challenges over to God, you surrender your ego's will and ask to be guided by Divine Love.

When you hand your challenges over to God, you display your absolute reliance upon Love.

You do not carry the weight alone.

Ramakrishna said, "God is in all men, but all men are not in God; that is why we suffer." He said, too, that absolute reliance on God "is the cessation of all anxieties and worries."

Why then, would you want to do anything without God?

God is Love, the light behind all that is, that which guides you in every moment, and that which loves you wholly as you are.

Asking Love to guide you in all matters releases the heavy weight of the burdens you carry.

Relying on Love to assist, direct, and support you relieves you of suffering and pain.

The way of the ego promises only sorrow, discontent, and despair.

But when you sincerely hand your burdens over to the Beloved, you can surrender into trust.

When you sincerely hand your burdens over to Love, you need not worry for even an instant.

The answers, assistance, and resolution you are seeking will come in time. If they have not yet arrived, it is not yet time to receive them.

Practice surrendering, one moment and one breath at a time.

Force is not the way.

Fear is not the way.

Hand your burdens over to God.

Allow yourself to be held through the pain, distress, and discomfort.

Allow yourself to be held in love.

Allow yourself to be guided by Love absolutely.

When you hand your hardships over to the Divine, you remember that you are not alone and need never navigate anything alone.

When you hand your hardships over to the Divine, you return to truth and the Ocean of Compassion available to assist you.

When you hand your challenges over to God, you remember that Love is always leading you home.

PEACE AND JOY
COME FROM WITHIN

"The Eternal is the treasure-house of real happiness."
—Anandamayi Ma

THE CENTER of your being is infinitely at peace and perpetually in love.

Peace and joy are inherent qualities of the soul; they are not given to you by the conditions of your external reality.

Life is a series of ups and downs.

That is how it is designed.

To constantly seek the pleasant, the pleasurable, and the pain-free, is to continuously be disappointed, dejected, and disheartened, over and over again.

To continuously seek peace and pleasure externally is a losing game, because both arise from within.

The habit of waiting for the next problem to appear is a trick of the ego, keeping you distracted and disconnected, keeping you in fear rather than love.

When the ego is driven by its desire for constant peace, denial, disappointment, and discontent become the norm.

When the ego's desire for constant pleasure rules, insanity ensues.

When you are firmly rooted in the Self, in your center, then what you are called to encounter is met with inner trust and peace.

When you are connected to Love, you are able to go wherever life takes you with faith. This does not mean there will be no pain, but rather that you will be able to navigate it with a deeper sense of acceptance and trust.

Connect to the space within you that remains completely untouched by the circumstances of your life.

Rest in the steady space within your heart that is a place of eternal peace.

Ground into the core of your being, the center of your heart, and the seat of your soul.

Rest in this space of unceasing bliss and boundless love.

The center of your being is completely and forever unaffected by that which arises and fades away within and all around you.

Directly above a sky full of clouds is a pure blue sky filled with radiant sunshine.

The perpetual sunshine is the Self and the clouds are the play of your incarnation.

The center of your being is your soul; it is Divine Love.

You can disconnect from Love and lose sight of it, but it will never disappear.

Even when darkness arrives, the sun continues to shine.

The truth of who you are is not at all touched by the unfolding of your reality.

Rest in the soul, that within you which is luminous peace, pure awareness, and eternal bliss.

Rest in the radiant, everlasting Love that you are.

THE ONLY RELATIONSHIPS YOU CAN CONTROL ARE THE ONES YOU HAVE WITH YOURSELF AND GOD

"Yesterday I was clever, so I wanted to change the world. Today I am wise, so I am changing myself." —Rumi

No MATTER how much effort you put into changing another, you cannot ultimately change them.

Your mind may tell you otherwise, but control is merely a dream of the ego.

A person can change only when the desire to do so arises from within.

A person can heal and grow only when the wish to do so is born from within their own being.

The only relationships you have power over are the ones you have with yourself and the Beloved.

You choose how to care for yourself in daily life.

You practice honoring and speaking up for your needs.

And it is you who chooses how to connect with and be in relationship with the Divine.

Attempting to change someone only breeds frustration, anger, and resentment, because the moment you let go of control, they simply return to who they have always been.

Every person in your life is exactly as they are to support your deepest healing and most expanded evolution.

When you feel the desire to change someone, reflect on how their soul may be supporting your own growth.

Are they supporting you in letting go of control, detaching with love, or redirecting your focus back to yourself?

Are they helping to teach you acceptance, trust, or surrender?

What is this person's purpose in your life?

Practice releasing the compulsion to control and return your focus back to yourself, as often as is needed.

Offer a prayer and ask for help.

You cannot control another, but you can control how you respond to others.

Bring your focus back to what you have power over—your relationship with yourself and Divine Love.

You can control how you care for yourself.

You can establish clear communication and set healthy boundaries.

You can create rituals that return you to truth and Love.

When you focus on others instead of yourself, you miss the opportunity to be present with your own experience.

You miss the opportunity to nurture and support yourself.

You miss the opportunity to tune into and honor what you most need.

While some relationships require significant attention and care, such as those between a parent and child, it is still essential for the caretaker to make time and space for themselves.

Every relationship benefits from you taking care of yourself physically, mentally, emotionally, and spiritually.

Every relationship in your life is nurtured when you prioritize your relationship with yourself and the Divine.

Your mind may give you reasons why this does not apply to you or your unique circumstances, but this is just illusion.

When you place your relationship with yourself and the Divine first, you create space to compassionately serve others.

When you place your relationship with yourself and the Divine first, you more easily practice acceptance and forgiveness.

When you place your relationship with yourself and the Divine first, you support the entire universe in returning home to Love.

YOU HAD THE FAMILY YOU NEEDED TO INITIATE YOUR SOUL'S JOURNEY IN THIS LIFETIME

"I submit to the mysterious force that is life, asking only that I be transformed into the perfect field of awareness through which love flows without obstruction." —The Way of the Heart

IN EVERY BIRTH, you receive the exact experiences you need to support the evolution of your soul, though they may not always be the ones your conscious mind desires.

This applies to all aspects of life, including your family and those who cared for you as a child.

You incarnated into the family and circumstances that would shape the lessons your soul came to experience, learn, and heal in this lifetime.

Your childhood experiences were entirely designed to support your deepest healing and most expanded evolution.

This is not meant to minimize the very real pain or harm that may have occurred, but rather to offer a way of perceiving your circumstances that can bring deeper meaning, peace, or purpose.

You may have been treated in certain ways or faced certain experiences that triggered the very wounds within that your soul came here to heal.

You were born into the family you needed in order to learn, love, and liberate yourself in the ways you took this birth to.

Parents, siblings, extended family, and beyond; every soul present to support your evolution in various ways.

Recognizing this often comes only after much healing has occurred, gradually, over time.

You need never force acceptance, meaning-making, or forgiveness.

There is never any rush.

May you honor, in each moment, the sacred pace at which you feel safe and able to move through your process.

Whether you felt deeply loved and held by your family, experienced deep pain within your family, or perhaps a combination of the two, there is divine purpose in it all.

Your parents and caregivers played the exact roles needed for your soul to get free.

Childhood can carry deep pain, yet this pain is never without purpose.

Through painful childhood experiences, the ways in which you came here to heal and the lessons you came to learn are set in motion.

Let it be clear that you did not deserve any pain or mistreatment.

It is rather that pain can powerfully support healing and a return to truth.

The pain was never meant to be a punishment; it came to open your heart and awaken something powerful within you.

The particular hardships of your childhood were placed upon your path to support the liberation of your soul, to support you in returning to your truest being, and to support you in returning home to Love.

Throughout your life, you will continue to work on the wounds of your childhood through your adult relationships, whether in partnership, parenting, friendship, or through your relationship with your pets.

Your soul's journey is initiated in childhood and continues to evolve throughout your incarnation.

You will revisit the same core themes, messages, and lessons on ever-deepening levels throughout your entire lifetime.

No matter the pain you may have experienced in childhood, you can trust there is sacred purpose woven deep within it.

The purpose may be to support you in loving yourself.

To support you in honoring the desires of your soul.

To help you stand in your power.

To teach you acceptance and patience.

To assist you in creating a loving home.

To prepare you to serve others.

To teach you forgiveness and unconditional love.

Pain arrived to pave the way to greater truth.

Pain arrived to help you set yourself free.

Every person in your family played the precise part needed to help you heal and grow in the ways you took this birth to.

Each person designed to support your remembrance and awakening.

Each soul placed upon your path to support you in returning to your heart and returning home to Love.

RELATIONSHIPS ARE A VEHICLE FOR THE EVOLUTION OF YOUR SOUL

"When you meet anyone, remember it is a holy encounter. As you see him, you will see yourself. As you treat him, you will treat yourself. As you think of him, you will think of yourself. Never forget this, for in him, you will find yourself or lose yourself."
—*A Course in Miracles*

THE RELATIONSHIPS in your life are vehicles for the evolution of your soul.

Every relationship, whether personal, professional, familial, casual, or intimate, exists to support your ultimate healing and growth.

Relationships help you release illusions of ego and return home to truth.

They teach compassion, forgiveness, and unconditional love.

Love means accepting people as they are.

The relationships in your life reflect where personal healing is needed and where your limits for love exist.

It is the nature of relationship to trigger your deepest wounds, so they may be healed.

Healthy and holy relationships require commitment and inner work.

Conscious effort is required to create safe and nourishing relationships.

Our world today holds a deeply skewed view of relationships, largely shaped by media rooted in ego. We have been told relationships exist merely to make us happy and that partners are here to fulfill us. This is not at all true and greatly minimizes the miraculous power of relationships and the profound evolution they can offer.

Relationships exist to return you home to truth and Love, which are the greatest gifts of all.

No one is here to fulfill all your needs or complete you.

No one is here to make you happy, for that is your work to do.

Relationships are twofold: they can provide profound safety, support, and connection, while activating your deepest wounds, as well.

Those you love will trigger the most wounded parts of you, and it is intentionally designed this way, not to hurt you, but to help you heal.

When someone leaves a relationship to avoid its challenges, they often continue attracting relationships with similar dynamics. They may wonder why the same themes and patterns continue to repeat, regardless of who they are with.

This is their soul desiring evolution.

This is Spirit offering them yet another opportunity to heal and grow.

The patterns continue until the lessons have been learned.

This is never punishment; it is only grace.

The soul is guided by the deep desire to return home to wholeness and truth.

Experiences that arise in relationships are divinely placed upon your path to support the evolution your soul desires.

A Course in Miracles teaches that heaven is entered two by two, meaning we cannot become free without one another.

It is other people who trigger you, teach you, and reflect yourself back to you.

It is others who help you access your feelings, act with compassion, and communicate respectfully.

It is through relationship that you learn to practice presence, honesty, forgiveness, acceptance, integrity, and love.

Through connection, your compassion deepens and your heart expands.

The experience of loss in relationship can bring you to your knees and cause tremendous suffering. And even this, as unbearable and earth-shattering as it can be, exists to assist you in your evolution.

Relationships illuminate all of the spaces within you that have forgotten truth and Love, so they may be brought into the light of awareness to be healed.

Being in a loving partnership offers the opportunity for profound inner work. Such work is known as relationship yoga.

Relationship yoga exists to bring you closer to the Divine.

Relationship yoga supports the evolution of each soul involved.

A healthy relationship is not one without conflict; it is one where conflict is moved through with humility, compassion, and respect.

It is about building the capacity, after a rupture, to resolve, repair, and reconnect.

A stable relationship requires commitment, effort, and the willingness to move through discomfort.

This does not mean there will be no joy, laughter, and love, but such gifts arise from a foundation rooted in commitment, truth, and trust.

Conflict is an opportunity for deeper healing and connection.

Secrets in relationship can create distance. There is a difference, however, between privacy, which supports well-being, and a secret, which can obstruct connection.

The healing power of gently sharing what you are feeling with another cannot be underestimated.

A single conversation has the power to release immense pressure within yourself and in a relationship.

Truth-telling is known to be one of the most difficult spiritual practices, and therefore, also one of the most purifying. The great challenge assists in profound purification on all levels.

Truth-telling cultivates greater courage, peace, and self-respect. It supports you in releasing attachments and fears, and living in alignment with divine will.

Sometimes communication is not met with the response the ego had hoped for, and that is okay.

Speaking your truth with vulnerability, honesty, and respect is something you do for yourself, the highest good of the relationship, and to take responsibility for your side of things. It is not about receiving a certain response, as much as the ego may desire one. The response you receive is ultimately the one that is needed at that moment in time.

When you cooperate with your evolution, you free yourself from having to experience louder and more painful calls for healing.

That being said, you are human, and the curriculum of relationships is a continuous learning journey, one that is ridden with mistakes, resolution, and repair.

Relationships are vehicles for the evolution of your soul, and while evolution is not always easy or comfortable, it is the very reason you are here.

Your external world reflects your internal world.

What arises externally is only here to support your healing within.

The relationships in your life are divinely designed to perpetually support your return home to Love.

INTERACTIONS WITH OTHERS EXIST TO SUPPORT YOUR EVOLUTION AND RETURN HOME TO LOVE

"Nothing is insignificant; everything has meaning."
—*Amma*

EVERY INTERACTION you have with another exists to support your healing, evolution, and return home to Love.

Perhaps you experience a brief moment with a stranger that profoundly supports you, such as someone who says the exact thing you need to hear during a short, unexpected exchange.

Or you may have an encounter with a stranger that is deeply triggering, such as a person who yells at you from their car while driving.

In both situations, the person and the interaction are precisely placed upon your path to support your learning, growth, and liberation.

Sometimes the purpose of the interaction is only visible in hindsight. Other times, it is clear in the moment.

You need not immediately understand how a particular interaction is meant to support you, but you can trust wholeheartedly that it is here to help you in some way.

This universe is built upon a foundation of love, and its purpose is always to return you home to Love.

When you are triggered by another, their soul is offering you a sacred opportunity to heal pain within.

When someone activates feelings of shame, anger, or frustration, those energies were already present within you.

The trigger brings them to the surface and into the light of awareness, which allows them to be acknowledged, felt, and eventually released from your emotional body.

Because this is an infinitely loving universe, you can trust that every interaction is guiding you back to truth, releasing you from the illusion of separation, and returning you home to the love that you are and the Love from which you came.

No matter the journey your soul is on, the interactions in your life exist with great purpose.

The perfection of the plan is beyond anything the human mind can fathom.

There is meaning in it all.

Every interaction in your life exists to bring you closer to the Divine.

Interactions may not always unfold the way your ego wishes they would, but they serve the exact role required for your evolution at that moment in time.

Even when a painful interaction occurs in your life, that too is here to help you.

This truth is not meant to bypass the pain or struggle such encounters can cause, but rather to invite reflection on how the people you meet exist to serve your learning, healing, and growth.

It is an invitation to shift how you perceive certain challenges that arise.

By trusting with every fiber of your being and every thread of the fabric of your soul that challenges exist to support your healing and evolution, you are able to rest in the faith that you are always exactly where you are meant to be.

You are divinely held, loved, and guided.

This is a loving universe, and the source of the universe is Love.

Your work here is to release illusion and return to truth.

While interactions with others may bring deep pain, shame, or struggle, they can also provide profound grace, support, and healing.

The people you encounter are divinely placed to help you remember.

They are mirrors.

They are teachers.

They are souls, perfectly placed to lead you to live in alignment with truth, courage, and compassion.

The people who appear in your life are part of a divine design to help you heal, grow, and return home to Love.

PRACTICE RESOLVING CONFLICT
WITH COMPASSION AND RESPECT

"A person who is not disturbed by happiness and distress and is steady in both is certainly eligible for liberation."
—Bhagavad Gita

THE PEOPLE in your life exist to support the evolution your soul desires.

The relationships in your life exist to support your deepest healing and most expanded growth.

Relationship challenges are opportunities to return home to truth and return home to Love.

Consistently avoiding conflict erodes authentic connection because each person's essential needs go unmet.

Learning how to meet and move through conflict with compassion and respect allows the relationship you have with yourself and others to flourish.

This can feel tremendously challenging because it goes against the experience your ego and nervous system are having in the moment, but it can become easier over time.

Learning how to tend to and regulate your nervous system during times of conflict greatly enhances your ability to move through activating situations with presence, honesty, and maturity.

Like forgiveness, resolving conflict from a balanced space is a skill you can learn, practice, and feel more comfortable with over time.

There are many ways to support yourself in doing so.

Offering a prayer before a difficult conversation can support you in navigating it with greater awareness and love.

Visualizing the conversation beforehand and seeing yourself acting in the precise ways needed can offer enormous support.

Taking slow, mindful breaths during the conflict supports you in remaining present and navigating the situation in alignment with love.

When conflict arises, know that you are exactly where you are supposed to be.

During conflict, you can pray, take a moment to pause and breathe, let the other person know you are stepping outside for a bit to gather yourself, or do anything else that supports you in grounding and reconnecting with truth and compassion.

The goal is to move from fear to love.

The goal is to be guided by the heart, not the ego.

When you speak the truth of your heart with respect, you honor both yourself and the other.

When you listen to what is being said and respond instead of react, you allow your heart and the heart of the other to feel safe.

Taking a deep breath before responding, and reminding yourself that you are triggered but safe, can be life-changing when moving through conflict.

Speaking about how you feel and focusing on how the situation affects you helps prevent you from blaming, shaming, or judging the other person.

Using discernment, rather than judgment, supports you in aligning with what is true without placing yourself above someone else, which is illusion.

Being guided by love may mean offering understanding.

Being guided by love may mean communicating your needs and setting boundaries.

You do not set boundaries to punish another. You set boundaries to support yourself in living a healthier life.

Practice setting the boundaries you need and want, and then practice honoring them.

Remember that every aspect of your life exists to support your healing and evolution. There is a reason that this conflict is arising at this exact moment in time.

How can you move through it with compassion?

How can you move through it with respect?

How can you communicate in alignment with love?

When conflict arises, acknowledge and feel the emotions it brings up.

Reflect on how this conflict is meant to support your healing and growth.

Take responsibility for your side of the street, as that is the only part that you have control over.

Get comfortable saying "I'm sorry," knowing that mistakes are simply part of being human and have no reflection upon your worth.

Practice having uncomfortable conversations from a grounded space.

Practice speaking up for what you need.

Practice sharing how the situation makes you feel, without needing to make the other person bad or wrong.

Be mindful of your volume and the manner in which you are expressing yourself.

Focus on your breath.

Remind yourself that you are safe.

Take space if it becomes difficult to remain grounded or if you need time to process any feelings on your own.

Remember, this is a life-long practice. You will not do any of it perfectly.

Life will continue to give you countless opportunities to practice.

It is possible to be firm without being aggressive.

It is possible to be honest without being critical.

But this way of being in the world requires patience, inner work, and courage.

This work is not easy, but it does become more familiar and natural over time.

The ego feels safer letting go the more its pain has been given adequate space to be seen and felt.

When you speak your truth, you act in alignment with the highest good of all souls.

When you honor the truth of your heart, you give others exactly what they need for their own soul evolution. Do not rob them of this opportunity.

When you take responsibility for your actions, acknowledge your blind spots, and remain open to what another shares during conflict, you allow yourself to align with truth and evolve in real time.

When you find yourself pushing up against another's ego, even while sharing from the heart, practice compassion, for they are hurting.

When you honor the truth of your heart, you may gravely disappoint or hurt the ego of another.

This does not at all mean you are doing the wrong thing; they are simply responding to the situation as best they can in the moment.

Breathe, pray, and honor your truth with compassion for the other.

Ask yourself, "What would love do?" and let the answer guide you.

Sometimes it will feel impossible to remember love in the midst of conflict, and that is okay.

Gradually with practice, we become better at recognizing and repairing the ways of the ego, as we allow ourselves to be guided by the ways of the soul instead.

This leaves us feeling better afterwards, with less guilt, shame, and blame, as we know we aligned our will with the will of the Divine, even under very challenging circumstances.

Whether the conflict is with a loved one or a stranger, it makes no difference. We are all neighbors in existence.

Every time you resolve conflict with love, you create greater peace in the world.

The conflicts that arise in your life are not punishments; they are invitations to heal in the exact ways your soul incarnated for.

Navigating and repairing conflict in alignment with your values strengthens your ability to love and trust yourself.

When conflict is navigated with loving awareness, the relationship can become stronger.

In relationships where each person is committed to navigating conflict with love, a solid foundation of safety and trust is built, upon which connection can deeply flourish.

Conflict is a natural part of human relationship.

Learning how to move through it with presence, compassion, and respect can profoundly deepen your connection with yourself and others.

When you align with love, you align with your true nature.

When you are grounded in the center of your being, you support all of existence in returning home to Love.

WHEN YOU HURT ANOTHER, YOU HURT A PART OF YOURSELF

"There are no others."
—Ramana Maharshi

WE ARE ALL ONE.

Each one of us a holy spark of the Divine.

When you harm another being, you not only hurt them, but you hurt a part of yourself as well.

We are all connected.

When you act in ways that are not grounded in compassion, you harm yourself.

Compassion is rooted in the knowing that we are all one.

Judgment, attack, control, gossip and manipulation each arise from the unprocessed pain of the ego.

The soul only leads with love.

When you hurt someone, you hurt yourself.

When someone hurts you, they also hurt themselves.

When you act out of alignment with love, you go against your true nature. What follows is often discomfort, a reminder that you momentarily slipped into the illusion of separation.

When you act in alignment with illusion, you block yourself off from Love.

When you act in alignment with love, you open yourself to ever-deepening Love.

When navigating challenging situations with others, we often seek support from someone we trust in order to process the situation.

However, there is a difference between processing from ego, with intention to feel superior, and processing from the heart, with intention to heal.

When someone triggers you, the feelings that arise are ultimately not about them; they are about you.

What arises within you is what calls for your attention. It was present before the trigger occurred and is now ready to be healed at a deeper layer.

The person who triggered you has presented you with a painful, yet valuable, opportunity to meet something within yourself—to meet this pain with presence and tenderness.

The feelings, stories, and beliefs that arise when triggered do so with great purpose. They are ready to be felt, acknowledged, and transformed.

They are ready to be released, one moment and one breath at a time.

Condemning another can temporarily relieve the ego of its own pain, but it does not support healing. It does not bring you closer to Love.

Judging others only delays the deeper work your soul came here to do.

The ego often criticizes others to relieve it of its own pain or shame. Though afterwards, you are left feeling worse, perhaps guilty or regretful, because this judgment is out of alignment with ultimate truth.

Through gossip, you bow to the illusion of separation.

When you catch yourself engaged in judgement of another, do not berate yourself. Judging yourself for judging another is merely the opposite side of the same coin. You are human, and actions born of forgetting are natural. Instead, offer yourself compassion, and allow the experience to support you in returning to love once again.

Practice becoming aware of how you speak about others. And first and foremost, practice being aware of how you speak about yourself.

The more you treat yourself with acceptance and compassion, the easier it becomes to offer that same love to others.

It feels infinitely better to speak kindly about another, to offer them understanding, and to respect the journey they are on than to speak ill of them.

Every behavior makes sense when we explore it deeply enough. When we reflect on how a person may have come to be a certain way, our understanding and kindness expand.

Take a moment to reflect on a time when you heard someone say something hurtful about you, or when someone spoke to you aggressively.

These moments can feel painful, frightening, or deeply shaming. They can create a sense of feeling unsafe and a longing to be held, cared for, and protected.

Now reflect on a time when you spoke to someone from anger or judgement.

You likely felt overwhelmed in that moment, reacting from a place of pain or fear.

You may not have realized what your words felt like to the person receiving them. You may not have seen how scared or hurt they were.

To be on either side of the experience feels awful.

It feels lonely, painful, and dark.

It feels terrible because it goes against your true nature, and the true nature of all beings—Love.

When you act from separation and the illusory belief that we are not all connected, you go against the current of Love.

You swim upstream.

You are left in a dream of duality and everything that is not real.

When you act in alignment with oneness, you are expanded, elevated, and supported.

You are guided, grounded, and blessed.

Your true nature is to care for yourself and others.

You were created to protect the unity between hearts.

Love is real.

Love is truth.

When you open your heart to love, you feel better.

Ground into love.

Be guided by love.

Lead with love.

When you align with love, your heart opens.

Your life and relationships open to greater love.

You step into deeper connection, greater truth, and grander joy.

Begin with yourself.

Speak kindly to yourself.

Treat yourself with understanding, gentleness, and care.

Your compassion must include yourself, or it is not anchored in truth.

Your love must include yourself, or else it is not true love.

Love does not exclude.

The more you practice accepting and loving yourself, the more you will naturally accept and love others.

Begin with yourself, and the ripples of that love will reach the heart of all beings.

LOVE DOES NOT EXCLUDE

"Never throw another out of your heart."
—Neem Karoli Baba

LOVE INCLUDES.

Love does not exclude.

Love is truth, and the truth is that we are all one.

We are each created of supreme truth, divine joy, and infinite Love.

We are each a ray of the same boundless, ecstatic light.

There is not a single soul excluded from this truth.

Not excluding another does not mean you cannot practice discernment and set boundaries around what is safe and healthy for you, but rather to never throw another out of your heart.

To offer compassion or understanding, even when someone causes pain.

It means not to banish them.

Not to exclude them from the field of love.

This is a practice that grows easier over time.

This is a practice that returns you to your truest being and the love that you truly are.

Love does not exclude.

Practice setting boundaries with love.

Communicating with love.

Using discernment with love.

Detaching with love.

You set boundaries for your own peace of mind, not to harm or punish another.

Your soul does not desire to judge, attack, or condemn.

Such behaviors are rooted in illusion and only pull you further into the dream of separation.

There is no energy you can be aware of in another that does not also exist within yourself.

Every being is born of the same radiant One.

We are all part of the same Divine Source, and we are here to learn how to recognize and treat each other as such.

When you exclude someone from your heart, you may be left with feelings of guilt, self-righteousness, or depression.

These feelings serve as signs that you have stepped out of alignment with your true being.

Love is the truth of who you are.

Love is the foundation of all of existence.

You were created to be grounded in love.

You were created to be guided by love.

When you feel hurt by another, first acknowledge the pain that arises within you and give your feelings the gift of your presence.

Honoring your feelings comes first.

Acceptance and forgiveness follow.

Not excluding someone does not mean that you condone their actions.

You may not at all agree with what someone has done, and yet you can simultaneously recognize that they are a human who is suffering.

You can see that they are a being created by the same universal, cosmic, and ethereal light as you.

You can practice loving their soul, not their role, and understanding that their soul is on its own journey.

Any suffering they cause for another creates karma they will one day have to face. In the end, they are only creating more pain for themselves.

Let this break your heart open.

Let this deepen the well of compassion within you.

The role this soul is playing in this lifetime is not who they truly are.

At their core, they are the same Divine Light as you.

We have all hurt others.

We can understand that our own suffering is what leads us to cause pain in another being.

Pain is born of suffering.

Hurt people hurt others.

You do not have to like another's ego, but you can practice seeing them as a soul.

You can practice feeling instead of judging.

And when you are ready, you can practice forgiving.

Everything will happen in divine timing, by God's grace.

The best way to learn how not to exclude is to practice being open-hearted with those your ego wants to reject.

Those who trigger your urge to exclude are here to support your healing.

They are here to support your forgiveness.

They are here to support your return home to Love.

All souls are equal in the eyes of Love.

Practice treating everyone you meet as your neighbor in existence.

Practice seeing all as the One, and the One in all.

This is the truth.

This is the way back home.

TREAT OTHER BEINGS AS YOU WISH TO BE TREATED, INCLUDING YOURSELF

"We learn how to accept the responsibility that we are all one consciousness in many bodies. We are one family."
—Ram Dass

TREAT EVERY BEING, whether person, plant, animal, and beyond, as you wish to be treated.

Begin first with how you treat yourself.

When you treat yourself with love, you support all of existence in returning home to Love.

We are all connected.

We are all one.

There is no difference between you and another.

There is no separation between the center of your being and the center of another's.

Navigate the situations that arise in your life with love.

This is not something you will do perfectly.

It is an ideal to consistently strive towards.

A north star.

Treat other beings as you wish to be treated.

Let love lead you.

Let love be your guide.

Ask yourself, "What would love do in this moment? How would love respond?"

When you act out of alignment with love, simply acknowledge what happened, repair the hurt, and do your best to do differently next time.

Be compassionate with yourself, for you are human, and mistakes are part of your journey here.

When you stray from love, it is an opportunity to offer yourself compassion and understanding.

When you realize you have strayed from love, it is an opportunity to return home to love once again.

Ask for help from the Divine.

You are not meant to do this alone.

When you try to, it is like swimming upstream.

You get nowhere.

But when you ask for help, Love guides you home.

When you act out of alignment with love, you may feel guilt, shame, or regret.

You may feel self-righteous, which is the ego's way of validating itself after separating from truth.

When you treat another being as you wish to be treated, you leave the interaction feeling connected to truth and love.

Your heart, open.

Your spirit, elevated.

Choosing love does not mean you avoid setting boundaries, speaking up, or using discernment, as these are necessary aspects of living a healthy life on this earthly plane.

But even when you do speak up or set a boundary, you do so with love.

With the awareness that there is no energy you can recognize in another that does not also exist within yourself.

With the humility to know you are not better or worse than anyone else.

You do not need to punish another or throw them out of your heart.

Practice treating others as you wish to be treated, whether they are physically in front of you or not.

Practice seeing others as they truly are, as manifestations of Love.

Practice being patient and accepting them as they are.

You are connected with all beings in existence.

When you hurt another, you hurt a part of yourself.

When you hurt yourself, everyone hurts with you.

There is not a single thought or action in your life that does not ripple out and affect the entire universe.

The way you speak to and treat yourself deeply matters.

You matter, and you impact all of existence.

When you treat yourself as you wish to be treated, you open your heart to acceptance, forgiveness, and peace.

When you treat others as you wish to be treated, you open your heart to unity and love.

When you treat others as you wish to be treated, you live in accordance with supreme bliss and your truest nature.

MIRACLES ARE NATURAL

"Miracles occur naturally as expressions of love. The real miracle is the love that inspires them." —A Course in Miracles

WHEN YOU TRULY UNDERSTAND WHAT a miracle is, you begin to recognize them everywhere.

A Course in Miracles teaches that miracles are natural; so natural that when they do not occur, something has gone wrong.

Fear, illusion, and separation can block miracles, but these are merely misperceptions of the mind.

They are not truth.

When you align with truth, miracles occur automatically and effortlessly.

The issue is not that miracles are not occurring; the issue is that you have not been taught to recognize them.

You live in a world where separation is mistaken for truth, and love is mistaken for illusion.

A miracle occurs every time you shift your perception from fear to love.

Anything that comes from love is a miracle.

With this understanding, you begin to see that miracles are happening all of the time.

A Course in Miracles also states that there is no order of difficulty when it comes to miracles, which means that a shift in your perception from fear to love is just as miraculous as a miracle that your ego might more easily recognize.

There is no hierarchy in the realm of miracles.

When you move from illusion to truth, it is a miracle.

When you move from separation to love, it is an absolute miracle.

The more you are able to recognize miracles in your daily life, the more you connect with the Love that you are, the Love from which you came, and the Love within and all around you.

Miracles are natural.

They return you to your truest being.

When you need a miracle, sincerely pray and Love will respond.

When you act with love, miracles are offered through you.

When you see through the fearful limitations of the mind, you recognize Divine Love as the essence of your being and the foundation of all of existence.

YOUR DREAM IS YOUR DESTINY

"The greatest tragedy in life is not death; the greatest tragedy takes place when our talents and capabilities are underutilized and allowed to rust while we are living."
—Amma

YOUR DREAMS and visions exist with immense purpose.

Your dreams are here to guide you exactly where you are meant to be.

The desires of your soul, not of the ego, exist to elevate and expand you.

They exist to release you from illusion and return you home to Love.

What brings peace and passion to your soul guides you towards that which you incarnated to experience and fulfill in this lifetime.

Every desire of your soul exists with reason.

When your mind attempts to steer you away from living the life you desire, pause, breathe, and remember that thoughts are not facts.

You are exactly where you are supposed to be.

Your current reality exists to support the desires of your soul.

Do not be guided by thoughts rooted in illusion, with foundations made of sand.

Allow yourself to be guided by the sacred, intuitive impulses within.

Allow yourself to be guided by God.

Your dreams will demand you to evolve.

They will push you, stretch you, and challenge you.

They will heal you, expand you, and transform you.

The dreams and desires of your soul require your healing and growth.

They require your courage, trust, and willingness to evolve.

Your evolution requires your active participation.

The desires of your soul exist to guide you home.

If you do not yet know where your soul longs to be, be patient. Surrender the need to know, for the answers will arrive in divine timing.

Every step along your path is preparing you.

Allow yourself to be guided by what feels aligned.

Let yourself be guided by truth.

Let yourself be guided by Love.

You are here to live the life you desire, and in doing so, you will inspire others to do the same.

Your destiny is your dharma, the roles and responsibilities you came here to fulfill.

The whole benefits when you honor your dharma.

The entire universe supports you when you walk in the direction of your destiny.

When you live your dharma, all of existence is supported.

When you live your destiny, you support all of existence in returning home to Love.

Challenges will come. Obstacles will arise. They are part of the path to pursuing your dreams.

You can move through them with trust and faith.

With commitment and responsibility.

Honor your dreams.

Honor the truth of your heart.

Honor the miracle that you are.

The universe is supporting and guiding you in each and every moment.

Your dharma is your dream.

Your dream is your destiny.

LET YOUR LIGHT SHINE

"Just be yourself. When you are yourself, you will be amazed how the universe takes care of you." —Robert Adams

EVERY PERSON in existence carries a divine essence.

Every person has a gift they can offer to the world, to support the collective in returning home to Love.

Each of us holds a unique brilliance, a spark of divinity within.

This spark is not meant to be hidden or hoarded.

It is meant to be shared.

And when it is, it always benefits the whole.

Let your light shine.

We need the miracle that you are.

We need the medicine of your open heart.

When you share from your heart, you help heal yourself and others.

We all receive a gift from the beauty of your being, from the magnificence of your truest essence.

There is no one who can be you better than you.

There is a unique expression of light that exists within you, and you alone.

You carry this light for us all.

The journey you are living in this lifetime is designed to help you recognize this light, honor this light, and share this light.

But it is essential to learn how to wield your light, as well, as a flame unharnessed can burn.

There is something original about you that only you can offer.

It matters not what you do or do not do for work.

What matters is the essence with which you move through the world and the light in your heart that you allow to shine.

What makes you *you* is wholly unique and gifted to you by the Divine.

The sacred parts of yourself that you could not get rid of even if you tried are the very gifts you came here to offer to the world.

All beings benefit when you share the truth, beauty, and love in your heart, because doing so leads them home to their true nature.

When you radiate the divine light within you, it inspires others to radiate the divine light within themselves.

Authenticity is divinely beautiful.

It is true, it is real, it is raw.

It is irreplaceable.

It is a treasure.

When you witness someone being authentic and sharing the light of their heart, you cannot look away.

It is magnetizing because it is real.

It is magnetizing because they are allowing Love to move through them unobstructed.

They are serving as a channel of the Divine.

They are mirroring back to you the desire of your soul to do the same.

Authenticity is living in alignment with your true Self.

A bird never silences its song for fear of who will hear it.

Any blocks that attempt to prevent you from sharing your light are the very blocks you came here to heal.

Ask for help and you shall receive it.

Be patient with yourself.

Trust your process.

There is no rush at all.

Easy does it, but do it. Go gently, but take inspired action when you can.

You are here to share the medicine of your open heart.

In doing so, you heal yourself and others.

Love is longing for the experience of being you.

You are a spark of the Divine expressing itself as you.

Let your life force flow through you unobstructed.

You traveled so far to be here.

Be who you are.

We need you.

We need the miracle that you are.

ON DEATH AND DYING

"Love is more powerful than death."
—Neem Karoli Baba

DEATH IS an inherent part of life.

You have died many times before, and you will meet death in this lifetime once again.

What is born must die.

What is never born, never dies.

It is only the ego that fears death, for in death it ceases to exist.

Death is a transition.

A most sacred ceremony.

Aging and death are holy practices in letting go.

Aging is a privilege.

Letting go is the essence of life.

The process of letting go of the ego's attachments prepares you well for the final process of letting go of this lifetime.

Life is a continual practice in releasing attachment and letting go.

Life is a continual practice in surrender.

You will only ever be asked to let go of that which no longer serves you, that which is transitory, or that which is illusion.

Doing so will only ever lead you home.

The great masters teach that when a person dies, it is neither a moment too soon nor a moment too late for their soul.

The timing is predetermined and precisely aligned for that particular incarnation.

Death allows the soul to continue on its evolutionary journey.

Death, both yours and that of another, invites you into surrender.

Death asks you to trust the great mystery and the love at the center of it all.

When the Divine determines it is time for your present incarnation to end, you will be invited to release all attachments of the ego and focus only on Love.

Speak the name of the Beloved, think of the Beloved, and desire only Love.

It is said this is how one eventually exits the endless wheel of life and death.

When it is your time to die, allow the grace of God to carry you.

Surrender into the arms of the Beloved.

Surrender into the bliss of Love.

Allow Supreme Truth to lead you home.

You have died before, and you will die once again.

The truth of who you are has never died.

The truth of who you are will never die.

Death is merely the dropping of the body.

You remain exactly as you truly are, always.

Death can bring great relief, comfort, freedom, and peace.

These bodies are ours on loan from the Divine.

They are not meant to last forever.

They are temporary vessels that allow the soul to navigate a particular human lifetime.

Death allows the journey of the soul to carry onward.

Death allows the soul to continue its evolution and journey home to Love.

Death is just another now moment.

Only the body dies.

The Self never dies.

The truth of who you are never dies.

The Love that you are remains, exactly as you are, forevermore.

TRUE LIBERATION OCCURS
THROUGH THE HEART

"The heart is the central point, the ultimate goal of all spiritual practice." —Anandamayi Ma

THE SEAT of the heart is the seat of the soul.

Evolution occurs through the heart because evolution is the process of returning home to Divine Love.

The heart center is the feeling center.

Your heart is a bridge between the physical and spiritual realms.

Healing can occur in the mind, but it does not occur through the mind.

The mind analyzes and interprets, labels and controls.

The heart simply knows.

The mind fears.

The heart trusts.

To the mind, truth is an idea.

To the heart, truth is felt.

The mind focuses on past and future.

The heart exists in the present moment.

Healing happens in the present moment.

Communication happens in the present moment.

Compassion happens in the present moment.

Forgiveness happens in the present moment.

Liberation happens in the present moment.

True healing occurs when you embody more love for yourself and others.

True transformation occurs not through thinking, but through feeling.

True transformation occurs through experiencing.

It is not information that returns you home to Love, but the embodiment of true wisdom.

Purification happens through the heart.

Devotion happens in the heart.

Sincere prayer is born from the heart.

Even if you read every book in existence, evolution would not be promised.

True liberation occurs through the heart because it is in the heart that you desire to accept, forgive, serve, honor, and love.

As the heart opens, fear dissolves.

As the heart opens, sight is returned to true vision.

When the heart is open, you embody the knowing that we are all one.

Freedom comes not from knowing wisdom, but from embodying it.

The mind is complex.

The heart is simple.

The heart is truth.

The heart is Love.

ON GRACE

"The winds of God's grace are always blowing, it is for us to raise our sails." —Ramakrishna

GRACE IS the unconditional love of the Beloved.

It is not something you earn; it is the love you receive for simply existing.

Grace is ever-present in the moments of your life.

Faith leads you towards grace.

Surrender leads you towards grace.

Grace cannot be controlled, only realized.

When you turn your vision towards grace through devotion, trust, or prayer, you begin to see it was there all along.

Grace is present in the everyday moments of your life.

Every new day you are given is the grace of God.

Every glass of water you drink is the grace of God.

Every meal you eat is the grace of God.

When you are present in the moment, that is Love's grace.

When you are present with your breath, that is Love's grace.

When you breathe, that is Love's grace.

Song is the grace of the Beloved.

Dance is the grace of the Beloved.

Laughter is the grace of the Beloved.

Action is grace.

Creation is grace.

Connection is grace.

Your ability to ask for help is the grace of the One.

Allowing yourself to receive support is the grace of the One.

Suffering that returns you home to Love is the grace of the One.

Synchronicities are God's grace.

An open heart is God's grace.

Your faith is God's grace.

Dreams full of wisdom are grace.

The desire to evolve is grace.

Miracles are grace.

The desire to remember your truest being is God's grace.

Grace is abundant in your connection with the natural world. Mother Earth, an extension and creation of the Divine, exists to ground, nurture, and support you. She exists to hold, heal, and nourish you.

When you appreciate the beauty all around you, that is the grace of the Beloved.

The awe you experience sitting under the evening sky is the grace of the Beloved.

The feeling you get sitting around an evening fire is the grace of the Beloved.

Sunshine is grace.

Plants are grace.

The elements are grace.

Nature is God's grace.

The abundance of the natural world is God's grace at play.

Grace is behind your loving actions in daily life. It is the reason you are able to heal, expand, and evolve.

When you accept yourself and others, that is the grace of the One.

When you are kind to yourself and others, that is the grace of the One.

When you forgive yourself and others, that is the grace of the One.

When you acknowledge, that is God's grace.

When you remember compassion, that is God's grace.

When you rest in your heart, that is God's grace.

When you trust yourself, that is grace.

When you are carried from fear to love, that is grace.

When you are firmly rooted in truth despite your circumstances, that is grace.

Your faith is Love's grace.

Your intuition is Love's grace.

Your surrender is Love's grace.

When you desire to be grounded in love, that is God's grace.

When you trust this is a loving universe, that is God's grace.

When you see the One in all, that is God's grace.

Grace is ever-present in your practices, always assisting your being in turning towards Love and deepening your devotion every day.

When you offer your thoughts to God, that is grace.

When you offer your feelings to God, that is grace.

When you offer your actions to God, that is grace.

When you sing in devotion, that is Love's grace.

When you meditate, that is Love's grace.

When you practice loving awareness, that is Love's grace.

Ritual, grace.

Ceremony, grace.

Prayer, grace.

Your body is God's grace.

Your life is God's grace.

Your soul is God's grace.

Your existence is God's grace.

The love you have for the Beloved is Love's grace guiding you home.

YOUR LIFE IS A DREAM THAT
EXISTS TO AWAKEN YOU

"It is all just a play. There is no question of that."
—*Anandamayi Ma*

YOUR REALITY IS a dream that exists to awaken you out of the illusion of separation.

Life is a game of hide and seek.

The Divine created you, hid itself within you, made you forget, and sent you on a quest to remember.

Your reality is a dream.

Your personality is a dream.

Your attachments are a dream.

It is all just a dream to help you awaken and return home to Love.

Practice letting go of attachments, for you do not need any where you truly are.

Only the transient ego has attachments.

The eternal soul is attached only and forever to Love.

You need nothing but Love when you return to wholeness.

You are connected to nothing but Love when you return to truth.

Your body was given to you by the Divine and is merely on loan for this one lifetime.

Bodies age and do not last forever.

You are not your body.

You are not your thoughts.

You are not what you have.

You are not what you do.

You are.

You simply are.

You are not the life you are living.

You are on an archetypal hero's journey, from one lifetime to the next.

Always heading in the same direction, towards home.

Your life is a dream that exists for the exaltation of Love.

Awaken in the dream.

Return to that which is true.

Return to that which is real.

Remember your true nature.

Remember love.

You exist, you have always existed, and you will never cease to exist.

You are Love.

Boundless, formless, timeless, and unending.

You are an aspect of the Beloved in form.

Everything is in you, and you are part of everything.

You are unchanging.

You are eternity.

You are the eternal.

EVERYTHING EXISTS TO
RETURN YOU HOME TO LOVE

"Supreme love is life's supreme goal."
—Neem Karoli Baba

EVERY ASPECT of your life exists with purpose.

Every experience that occurs throughout the day, whether internal or external, exists to return you home to Love.

Your life is a vehicle through which you are evolving.

This is an infinitely loving universe.

The foundation of all of existence is Love, so it must be true that what transpires in your life exists to return you home to Love.

Everything that unfolds is here to help you heal and grow in the ways your soul incarnated for, to support you in remembering the truth of who you are, and to awaken you to your true nature.

You are a child of God.

Challenges exist to help you heal precisely what you took this birth to heal.

The universe is always supporting you in living the highest octave of your sacred incarnation.

The universe is always working to help you dissolve illusion and return to truth.

Allow this knowing to fill your heart with faith, trust, and surrender.

You are always exactly where you are meant to be.

You do not have to make sense of everything.

You do not have to have all the answers.

You do not have to know or understand what comes next.

Simply trust in that which created you.

Trust in that which carries you.

Allow yourself to be guided by Love.

Ground into faith that everything is arising to support you in healing and growing in the exact ways your soul desires.

Let Love lead you, one moment and one breath at a time.

Trust where you are being led and know that everything is guiding you home.

This does not mean the journey is free from pain. There is pain, and that, too, exists to bring you closer to that which is eternal.

Feel your feelings.

Every time you allow yourself to feel, you receive a healing and support the evolution of your soul.

Ask for help, from God and others.

When you are navigating challenges or pain, hold on to the knowing that everything exists to return you home to Love. This is never to avoid the pain, but to ground yourself in trust and faith while moving through it.

This truth will transform your life.

It will help you embody greater acceptance, trust, and surrender.

Your experience of peace, Spirit, and miracles will expand.

A miracle occurs every time you shift your perception from fear to love.

Everything that comes from love is a miracle.

Miracles are natural. They occur often; you simply were not taught to see them before. But now, you will be able to recognize them.

Healing is a spiral, an ongoing process.

Your evolution continues, forever moving you closer and closer, inch by inch, bit by bit, to being fully awakened, fully realized, and fully embodied as the Love that you are.

Love exists within and all around you.

Everything occurs with purpose, including every frustration, obstacle, and hardship that arises.

Even when something does not appear to hold a thread of hope or meaning, you can be certain the Divine is carrying you through it with purpose.

This is all a dream designed to awaken you to your holiness, courage, and compassion.

Lead with humility, integrity, and honesty.

Live your dharma.

Allow your surrender.

Practice acceptance and forgiveness, for yourself and others.

Every moment of your life is divinely guided to assist you.

The circumstances of your life are perfectly designed to support your return home to Love.

You are exactly where you are meant to be.

You are held.

You are cared for.

And you are being guided.

You are a pure, radiant spark of the Divine.

You are source incarnate.

We need you.

We need the miracle that you are.

We need the medicine of your open heart.

You are a masterpiece.

You are a treasure.

You are the song of the Beloved.

Thank you for being here.

Thank you for being you.

This is a loving universe.

All of existence loves you.

You are being carried by Love, for Love, and with love.

Allow yourself to awaken to the Love of your truest being.

Allow yourself to be embraced by the Love that guides you.

Allow yourself to be enveloped in the love that you are.

Every single moment offers an opportunity for your awakening.

Every moment of your life exists to return you home to Love.

EPILOGUE

May you find immense solace in knowing that this great mystery
is profoundly and powerfully rooted in love.

May you walk with continual acceptance knowing that
everything happens with purpose and reason.

May you surrender with deep trust in knowing that the core of
all of existence is Love.

May you let go with effortless ease in the knowing that Love will
always and forever guide you gracefully home.

PRAYERS

The following are prayers and mantras you can work with whenever you wish. You can also speak any prayers, intentions, or mantras alive in your heart at any time.

~

May I be who you want me to be,
May I go where you want me to go,
May I do what you want me to do,
May I see how you want me to see,
May I live the life you want for me.

~

May I be grounded in love,
May I be guided by love,
May I lead with love.

~

May I be grounded in you in all that I do.
May I be guided by you in all that I do.

≁

I pray to keep my heart open, even in the
moments when it wants to close.

≁

May I go beyond the thoughts of the mind
and rest in the seat of the soul.

≁

May I surrender to the evolution my soul desires.

≁

May I open to the Love within and all around me.

≁

Please guide me to live your will for me.

≁

Please help me live in alignment with integrity and truth.

≁

My presence and slowness are my devotion.

≁

I trust, surrender, and offer myself to the Beloved.

∾

May I do as Love would have me do.
May I be as Love would have me be.

∾

Fear is illusion; love is real.

∾

I am a manifestation of God and I love myself.

∾

Please help me remember you today.

∾

I offer my thoughts, actions, and life to you today.

∾

May I be a vessel for Love.
May I be a vessel of love.

∾

May I be guided by you in all that I do.
I offer my whole life to you.

∾

I bow to the sacred
I bow to the Divine
I bow to Love.

~

May my awareness of the Divine Love
that I am deepen every day.

~

I offer my actions to you, Beloved, and release all attachment to the
results.

~

May my thoughts, words, and actions
be rooted in love.

~

May I move throughout the day rooted in
the center of my being that is pure Love.

~

May I know truth and Love,
May I see truth and Love,
May I be only truth and Love.

~

May each breath carry me deeper into the Love that I am.

~

I surrender into Love and allow myself to be moved by Love. I breathe, trust, and let go.

ALL HAIL LOVE
Ram Ram

A PRAYER FOR ALL BEINGS

A prayer for our family of all beings, everywhere. You can recite this whenever you feel called to offer love and support to those who are suffering.

My heart beats within you, and yours within me.
We have the heartbeat of the entire universe within us.
May you be safe.
May you be free from harm.
May you have a comfortable place to rest.
May you be well nourished and cared for.
May you be tenderly held through any pain.
May any suffering you endure lead you directly to the Divine.
May you be swiftly carried back to peace.
May you be swiftly carried home to Love.
May you find your way back to the Divine Joy at the
center of your being.
May you find your way back to the Eternal Love that you are.

SUGGESTED READING

The following are books filled with sacred wisdom that may resonate for you, should you feel called to dive in deeper to any of these teachers or teachings.

A Course in Miracles by Foundation for Inner Peace

A Goddess Among Us: The Divine Life of Anandamayi Ma by Swami Mangalananda

Autobiography of a Yogi by Paramahansa Yogananda

Be Love Now: The Path of the Heart by Ram Dass and Rameshwar Das

Bhagavad Gita, various translations exist. The Stephen Mitchell translation is a wonderful edition to begin with, though you can explore other versions to see which resonate most.

Chants of a Lifetime: Searching for a Heart of Gold by Krishna Das

Letters from Sri Ramanasramam Volumes I & II by Suri Nagamma

Miracle of Love: Stories About Neem Karoli Baba by Ram Dass

Paths to God: Living the Bhagavad Gita by Ram Dass

Ramakrishna as We Saw Him by Swami Chetanananda

Ramayana, many translations exist. The original Valmiki Ramayana, the Tulsidas Ramayana (*Ramcharitmanas*), and William Buck's English translation are widely read editions. *Sita's Fire* by Vrinda Sheth is a modern retelling of the Ramayana from Sita's perspective. It honors the divine feminine and illuminates Sita's strength, wisdom, and depth. You can explore different versions and see which ones resonate most for you.

Sri Siddhi Ma: The Story of Neem Karoli Baba's Spiritual Legacy by Jaya Prasada

Talks with Sri Ramana Maharshi by Munagala Venkataramiah

The Essential Sri Anandamayi Ma: Life and Teachings of a 20th Century Saint from India by Anandamayi Ma and Alexander Lipski

The Gospel of Sri Ramakrishna by Swami Nikhilananda

The Way of Mastery (Parts One – Three) by the Shanti Christo Foundation

Walking Each Other Home: Conversations on Loving and Dying by Ram Dass and Mirabai Bush

Words of Sri Anandamayi Ma compiled and translated by Atmananda

Whisper in the Heart: The Ongoing Presence of Neem Karoli Baba by Parvati Markus

ACKNOWLEDGMENTS

Thank you, Deborah Hanekamp, for seeing me writing this book, initiating me onto the path of writing it, and guiding me deeper into my dharma. Thank you, Kristen Paige Andrews, for the beautiful cover design, Rachel Warmath for editorial support, and Aaron Reppert for editing and mastering the audiobook.

Thank you, Michael, for assisting with this creation and for your love. Nala, you are perfect. Thank you for being in my life. Thank you to my family for all your love and support, and thank you, Marilyn and Lenny, for your warmth and generosity.

Thank you to my teachers, including Neem Karoli Baba, Anandamayi Ma, Ramakrishna, Ramana Maharshi, Amma, Ram Dass, Krishna Das, Nina Rao, Michelle Dench, and Ari Moshe Wolfe.

Hanuman, you are the Ocean of Compassion, Remover of Obstacles, and the Remover of Darkness. You blessed and guided this entire movement of creation from beginning to end. It is all your grace; it is all yours. Thank you, thank you, thank you.

Thank you to every person, being, and spirit who has lovingly supported me on my path.

Thank you to the souls I have had the privilege of working with, connecting with, and growing with through my work.

Thank you to the animals, elements, and sky above for nourishing and enriching my life.

And to you, the one who is reading this: thank you for welcoming this book and its teachings into your life. Thank you for being you. Thank you for the love that you are and the love that you offer to this world.

To those I have met and to those I have not: we are all one consciousness in many forms. We are one spiritual family. We are one.

We are the One.

Thank you, all.

Thank you, God.

With You in the Field of Love,

Brooke

ABOUT THE AUTHOR

Brooke's life is in devotion to Divine Love.

She has been a therapist for over a decade and specializes in Brainspotting and psychedelic therapy.

Her dharma is to help others remember the love at the center of their being and all of existence.

She loves animals, singing, and nature.